BRING OUT TI...
AND YOUR FAMILY WITH THE TIMELY
WIT AND WISDOM OF
ABCs OF REAL FAMILY VALUES:

Here's a small sampling of the simple values you'll read about in these pages:

A is for Affection:
"Like a little tap on the shoulder, affection reminds us that virtue springs from love."

B is for Babying Babies:
"Babies cry simply because they are hungry or uncomfortable or scared. If we don't pick them up immediately the only thing they experience is more hunger, more discomfort, more fear—and are less likely to be trusting when they finally do have thoughts in their heads."

C is for Chaos:
"Disorder is the order of the day in any normal family. Just look around. I know it's hard to believe, but I have discovered that children sometimes do not do as they're told."

D is for Discipline:
"Because I say so is a staple in our parental lexicon not because we love power, but because we've learned that it's exactly the answer that our children want to hear."

STEVEN LEWIS, author of *Zen and the Art of Fatherhood*, has written on family issues for the *New York Times*, *Los Angeles Times*, and *Parenting*, as well as numerous other national magazines and newspapers. A father of seven children, he is a professor of English and Literature at Empire State College in New Paltz, New York.

Also by Steven Lewis

Zen and the Art of Fatherhood

The ABCs of Real Family Values

The Simple Things That Make Families Work

STEVEN LEWIS

A PLUME BOOK

For my parents,
Lillian Aaronson Lewis
Samuel Ira Lewis

PLUME
Published by the Penguin Group
Penguin Putnam Inc., 375 Hudson Street,
New York, New York 10014, U.S.A.
Penguin Books Ltd, 27 Wrights Lane,
London W8 5TZ, England
Penguin Books Australia Ltd, Ringwood,
Victoria, Australia
Penguin Books Canada Ltd, 10 Alcorn Avenue,
Toronto, Ontario, Canada M4V 3B2
Penguin Books (N.Z.) Ltd, 182–190 Wairau Road,
Auckland 10, New Zealand

Penguin Books Ltd, Registered Offices:
Harmondsworth, Middlesex, England

First published by Plume, an imprint of Dutton NAL,
a member of Penguin Putnam Inc.

First Printing, June, 1998
10 9 8 7 6 5 4 3 2 1

 REGISTERED TRADEMARK—MARCA REGISTRADA

LIBRARY OF CONGRESS CATALOGING-IN-PUBLICATION DATA:

Lewis, Steven M.
    The ABCs of real family values : the simple things that make
families work / Steven Lewis.
        p.   cm.
    ISBN 0-452-27860-0 (alk. paper)
    1. Child rearing.   2. Family.   3. Values.   I. Title.
HQ769.L422 1998   97-49946
306.85—dc21   CIP

Printed in the United States of America
Set in Palatino
Designed by Leonard Telesca

When I'm Old And Gray

When I'm old and gray I'll say renember when I was a little girl. When I skiped around the fire ring. When my voice sounded like a blue jay. When I was full of energy. When I felt graet. When I was cold I would snugle close to my momma and dadda. When I would put my dolls to sleep. I will renember those days when I was a girl.

—Elizabeth Bayou-Grace Lewis, seven years old

Contents

Introduction

Some old friends of ours had a bumper sticker on their Volvo station wagon that read: IT'S NOT EASY BEING A PARENT.

Everyone who has ever had children—or is in the last few steps of a mountainous pregnancy—knows in the stretched fibers of their aching muscles just how hard parenting can be. Yet I was always a little irked by that sad phrase whenever we pulled up behind our friends' car in the driveway. I remembered what Scott Peck has observed so wisely: "Life is hard," not just parenting. It's also hard to be a dentist or a factory worker or a secretary or a CEO or a teacher. It's hard to be sick. It's hard to be old. It's hard to be virtuous. And, as anyone who has ever been a child knows, it's always hard to be a kid.

But I was irked, too, because that bumper sticker told only a small part of the bigger truth—it's the Oreo without the filling. On each visit, before we got out of the van and walked up the bluestone path to their cottage, I was tempted to pull out a magic marker and scribble right on the bumper: BUT CHILDREN HELP TO SOFTEN THE BLOW.

Despite all the well-publicized hand-wringing, hair-pulling, vein-popping *agita* that parents of all

shapes and ages endure while raising children of all disposi-
tions and magical powers of manipulation, there is nothing in
the cold, hard universe to give a person a softer soul—and a
cushier landing—than a child. Children show us how to make
water slides of muddied lawns, how to take disappointment
with a grain of salt (and a soupspoonful of sugar), and how to
bridge the great chasms between generations by reminding us
of the very same values our parents handed down to help us
survive the hard days and cold nights. Hanging on to our
apron strings or belt loops, feet flying out the windows, sticky
fingers grabbing for the brass ring, children orbit around the
scary cosmos giving their hapless parents purpose, perspective,
love, comfort, and, just when we need it, a great laugh. In valuing us, they give us value. And in giving us value, they spur us
to provide values to live by.

As a father of seven mostly wholesome kids, I've spent much
of the last twenty-eight years in awe of the ways that real children and real families live their lives in remarkably virtuous
ways. Although in recent times *family values* has become a political football tossed around the country like a kids' game of
keep-away, I haven't seen much evidence of the breakdown
that our public figures seem to worry so much about. When I
was a child on Long Island in the storied fifties, PTA and Board
of Education meetings were nearly as poorly attended and
impassive as school soccer games (where we often had no spec-
tators). Now try getting a seat—or a word in edgewise—as concerned parents cram into school meetings demanding more
and better for their children. Try getting a front-row position on
a worn youth soccer field lined with beach chairs. Try finding a
parking spot at the local church or synagogue to attend SRO
services.

Of course, the contemporary household does not look very
much like the frozen images of families from fifty or a hundred
years ago. We'd be hard-pressed to find any clan like the Ingalls
or the Waltons—or Ozzie and Harriet and their boys—in a
minivan cruising down Main Street or up Broadway in 1998.
(In truth, I suspect that the Ingalls, the Waltons, and the Nel-

sons would not resemble their own idealized images at all.)
Over the past several years—and miles and miles of concrete—
the definition of family has been stretched and molded and
sleekly remodeled in ways that make it appear somewhat different than ever before. Yet the family still serves the same purpose as it always has: to guide children from helpless infancy to
responsible self-sufficiency. And mostly it works, just as it
always has. Mostly I've seen parents doing their level best to
keep their bobbled heads on straight as they navigate (lead, follow, push, drag) their kids safely across the busy streets of
modern life. And, once safely on the other side, to try to enjoy
some well-earned peace and quiet (and maybe a glass of champagne).

In 1969, my oldest son, Cael, entered the universe wailing for
food and immediately transformed the notion of family values
for my wife, Patti, and me from a vague political concept to a
virtuous reason to wake up several times in the middle of the
night—and then again early the next morning. Four years later,
Nancy emerged to teach us, among many other things, the real
issues involved in fidelity. And two years after Nancy, Addie
arrived to school us in spirit (and a dose of contentiousness).
Another two years passed and Clover brought along a living
slide show on justice; and in 1979 Danny first demonstrated his
unique approach to learning manners at the family table. By
1985, just as Patti and I thought we knew everything there was
to know about family values, Bay knocked at the door to
deliver some lectures on presence; and three years later, when
we should have been just about ready to hang up the parenting
shoulder pads, Elizabeth appeared like a light in the window,
to show us just how much we still have to learn about making
a home.

The ABCs of Real Family Values is not filled with worried pre-
dictions about the dissolution of the family. It's not about idealized family life, not politically correct family life, not TV
family life, not "back in the good old days" family life. This
book is a celebration of the eternal values that come to light
through the daily lives of real mothers and fathers and chil-

dren. It is filled with the stories of real family life that get told over and over again on the front porch or the front stoop or across the kitchen table, until your sides ache from laughing or your eyes sting from tears. It is the ABC's of life as we do, not as we say. And it is the way we gather 'round each other to soften the blows of life, just as the traditional lullaby has soothed babies for generations. If that mockingbird don't sing, Daddy (or Mama or brother or Aunt Leigh or cousin Peter) will get you a golden ring. And if that golden ring turns brass—and the lookin' glass gets broke—and the billy goat don't pull—and the dog named Rover don't bark—and the horse and cart fall down . . . if everything gets so hard it hurts . . . your family will still make you feel like the cutest—and most valued—little boy or girl in town.

Over my desk hangs a yellowed and wrinkled pencil drawing of a big Indian and a little Indian. At the top of the paper in elementary school scrawl it says, "Like Father Like Son." Danny, who is now eighteen, made that drawing for me nearly a dozen years ago. I keep it in front of me to this day not only because it makes me feel good whenever it catches my eye, but because it reminds me how a child can see the eternal goodness—and rightness—in a father who doesn't always see it so clearly in himself. It makes me laugh. It gives me faith.

And it is in that spirit that I offer these testaments to the resilient—and wonderfully quirky—virtues of real family life. Have faith.

Affection:
Where Virtue Is Born

Devils can be driven out of the heart by the touch
of a hand on a hand.
——Tennessee Williams,
The Milk Train Doesn't Stop Here Anymore

In the beginning of all beginnings, there is that
one exclusive and private moment when the most
sincere sperm wriggles and jiggles its way
through the thin-as-linen membrane of the first
demure egg in the ovarian line. Everything is
silent. Everything is still. Everything is necessarily as it should be.

Seconds later, though, the bright house lights go
up with a *thunk,* and the audience in a giant
amphitheater stands and cheers the startled couple who thought they were alone in the midst of
some transcendent dream.

And from that starkly public moment forward,
the two lovers are never again unaccompanied in
their shared joy. Outside the theater, walking

down the street, standing in line at the supermarket, it seems that everyone's got a comment, a warning, a story, a superstition, a scientific fact, a knowing smile, a pat on the shoulder, a touch of the belly, a talisman, a friend, a book, an herb, a doctor named Herb. And they're all experts on babies. And then toddlers. And then preadolescents. And then the quantum leap: moody, unrepentent teenagers.

The deluge of advice on childrearing is overwhelming to any new parent preparing to bring a tiny infant into the community of others; or, for that matter, any couple already staggering under the weight of several kids, a mortgage, sticky floors, a mountain of laundry, and chronic lack of sleep. Yet, in all the years Patti and I have been trying to keep this weathered houseboat afloat with seven kids (dogs, cats, rabbits, ducks, goats, guinea pigs, lizards, fish, and the occasional orphaned friend), no one has ever offered up what is perhaps the most important family value in raising moral, seaworthy children: Affection.

So I begin this book with Affection, not only because it starts with the letter A (a remarkably fortunate coincidence), but also because, without genuine affection in a family, all other values and virtues are rendered meaningless. (Don't worry, I'm not advocating smarmy group hugs for all. In my vision of family life, you can hug gooey or sweaty relatives without actually touching them.)

A loving touch was the first subject I considered when writing *Zen and the Art of Fatherhood*. And the opening chapter of that book was about my fifties father, who, like most of the men in the neighborhood, worked long and hard and consequently had precious little time for the games of little boys. We didn't go fishing together or shoot hoops or just lie out under the stars and talk about girls, punchball, eternity, or girls. We were not pals. But whenever my dad and I rode together in the car, he would reach across the long bench seat in the Chevy station wagon and hold my hand. He wouldn't say anything, I don't even remember him looking my way, but his rough hand on mine was enough to let me know that he loved me. That I was valued. Everything else—all the fun stuff of fatherhood that I've been lucky enough to share with my own kids—was just gravy. I had other people more my age to play with me. But I could walk out the door of my house every day safe in the knowledge that I was wanted and loved.

Over the past twenty-eight extraordinary, unpredictable years—a story I never could have written had I not lived it—I have come to see my big family as a ragtag team in a ten-legged race hobbling across a large meadow. Tied at the ankles with brightly colored bandanas and held up by arms wrapped around each other's unequal shoulders, we stumble ahead—though often to the side and occasionally backwards—trying desperately to find the right balance and cadence that will take us all the way to the finish line. Standing up, that is. Sometimes we fall in a jumbled heap of torsos. Sometimes we laugh like orangutans, arms and legs twisted around each other so that you can't tell which limb belongs to whom. Sometimes we howl in anger and pain like wounded wolves. And sometimes we just weep like the children we always are. But it seems we always hold on affectionately—desperately—to the family member on one side and help the one on the other side to get up. We hold each other up. We touch each other's soul so that our bodies can move along to do what each of us must to feel whole. We heal each other with our hands. It's not always pretty, and it's not always fun, but it always gets us to where we want to go. Here. Now.

Of course, affection comes in all forms. Since the family starts with Patti and me, I'll start with holding hands. Of all the connections we have—and Patti and I have connections that go back beyond the tenderhearted bed, beneath the sensuous and fertile bayou, indeed deep into the darkest depths of the prehistoric cave—there is no touch in the universe that makes me feel as whole as holding hands with my soul's mate. On the street. On the beach. In the woods. But mostly in the movies. In the cinematic darkness we are linked finger through finger against the limits of time, space, politics, and mythology, palm pressed against palm, the storied history of the world flashing before our amused eyes. Everything follows from that.

And from there, each of the kids have touched me in their own unique way. I remember being twenty-three and rocking Cael to sleep one night in 1969, stunned that I was old enough to be someone's daddy and suddenly realizing that time slips away so quickly I should remember exactly how he looked at that moment. Nearly twenty-eight years later, though, which feels like a week and a half, that tiny baby is over six feet tall and weighs 190 pounds. And, of course, I can't see his baby face very clearly; nor can I visualize the closet-sized nursery or the footed pajamas he had on. But I can still feel the weight of my little boy in my lap, recall the fineness of his hair, the shape of his tiny skull.

When Nancy, who is now twenty-four, was a roly-poly baby of beachball dimensions, she would bury her little bald head into the cave of my arm whenever she was distressed. That was the way she fell asleep. And I can still feel her warm breath on my chest whenever the world turns cold. As I can feel twelve-year old Addie's arm through mine as we walk along the roiled surf in Hatteras; or at eighteen down a cobbled street in Taxco; and at twenty-one in Barcelona. Her arm through mine.

I was the first one in the universe to touch Clover, born into my trembling hands upstairs in the yellow wallpapered bedroom of the brick farmhouse on Coffey Lane in 1977. Her imprint is there whenever I open my palms to the sky.

As it is still there, in light pink and tints of blue, right where eighteen-year-old Danny punched me in the arm last night when we were doing the ancient punch for punch dance, pretending not to be staggered by the other's shot. For those of you who have teenage boys, you'll understand the deep affection that goes into fathers wrestling and sparring with their boys. But Danny also touches me when he asks about my day—and genuinely wants to know how it went.

Bay, who at eleven has not yet felt the need to bump chests against the old man, leans into me on the couch, holds onto my shirtsleeves at bedtime, and allows me to hold his hand when we ride in the car. I sometimes think that I can feel my father's calloused palm on my left hand as I steer down Springtown Road, my mitt on Bay's thick boyish paw.

And then there's the baby, Elizabeth Bayou-Grace, nine, who laces her elegant, thin fingers in mine as we cross the street— still showing me how to be her dad.

To complete the circle is Cael again, who, even though he lives five states away, still calls sometimes in the middle of the day. Not because he loves me or needs my advice, but mostly because he's bored at work. It doesn't matter, though; I can feel him leaning next to me when he phones. That, too, is a touch.

It drives out the devils. Like a little tap on the shoulder, affection reminds us that virtue springs from love.

Advice:

Its Value in the Family Bond Market

> I have found the best way to give advice to your children is to find out what they want and then advise them to do it.
>
> —Harry Truman

Danny's brown eyes are rolling upward into the adult-resistant recesses of his hard skull. The look on his sculpted adolescent face, which is seen only if you bend down and look under the emphatically rounded brim of a heavily soiled baseball cap, is one of pure emptiness. It is, I believe, a teenage form of selective catatonia that is triggered by the noxious lecturing tone of an adult life form in his presence.

Unfortunately, I happen to be the adult this time—though it could just as easily be a high school teacher droning on about the merits of organized note-taking, or an old lady at the Plaza Diner tsk-tsking about hats and manners and disrespectful kids *these days,* or perhaps an anal-retentive vegan on Main Street rabidly discussing the twin hazards of eating flesh (aggression and bowel cancer). In fact, the virtual human being in front of me doesn't have to be Danny; it could be someone else's seventeen-year-old kid with the bored scowl on his face. It really doesn't matter; he's not listening anyway. He's *been there* thousands of times.

Nevertheless, since I ostensibly have your attention (if not his), the subject of this particular early-senior-year lecture concerns his homework. It is the tip of the iceberg that also involves achieving good grades, preparing for the SATs, and getting into the college of his most Bacchanalian dreams. Not too complicated. The simple message that I think I'm replaying for my fifth seventeen-year-old is the old Norman Vincent Peale standby about personal empowerment, taking charge of his own destiny, not settling for mediocrity, grabbing the brass ring. (Translation: Listen to me, I'm your father, I know best.)

His response? Out of the fog of temporary dementia he barely utters the two words that never fail to make the paternal blood boil—"I know"—or the more contemptuous three-word zinger: "I know"—insert lengthy pause—"Dad." (Translation: You're a much bigger fool than I ever imagined possible.)

"If you know, then why don't you do it?" I snap back, totally decomposed. With due deference to Hamlet, *that* is the real question, not some abstract query about the nature of existence.

But Danny doesn't have an answer for me. He smiles a little sheepishly under the shadowy brim and shrugs. And while I'll admit that I'm thankful for the sheepishness—any morsel of evidence that I'm still a force in his life is gratefully acknowledged—I'm still perplexed. As Robert Fulghum reminded us some years back, Danny learned just about everything he ever needed to know way back in kindergarten. He knows that he *should* do his homework and get good grades, just as he knows that he *should* be polite and he *should* do his chores and he *should* go to sleep at a reasonable hour so he can get to school on time—which he *should* do every day. In truth, he also picked up a few important lessons after he graduated cum laude from kindergarten, like he *shouldn't* drive over the speed limit, he *shouldn't* look at girls solely in sexual terms, he *shouldn't* drink beer, and, most of all, he *shouldn't* blow off the sage advice of his father. All of which is to say that he shouldn't act like I did when I was a teenager.

Which is why I'm finally beginning to suspect that the giving of advice in most real families is worth little more than the hot air it takes to expel it from one's parentally clogged cranium. The world is suffering from chronic advice syndrome. And nobody is listening! Which is why all those sweet smiley-face morality tales of sharing in nursery schools are exercises in futility. (Who has ever met a healthy toddler who is able to share without an adult police presence?) And what about those Official Rules pamphlets that school districts dispense each September? (Is there one child—or one parent—who reads them?) And those expensive Madison Avenue public service ads to protect teenagers from sex, drugs, and rock 'n' roll? (Laughable, at best.)

Of course, we adults love to serve up advice as if we're oracles of reason and wisdom. Whether we employ the traditional caffeine rant (bulging eyes-rubber bands in neck-finger pointing-frothing at the mouth)—or New Age herbal (hand on shoulder-nodding head-*I feel your pain*), standard parental counsel seems only to serve the ones who are doing all the talking, the ones who embrace the devoutly adolescent illusion that they would actually follow their own advice.

If there is a universal truth about the value of advice in real families, it is that children have to make the right choices for themselves, or those non-choices become the equivalent of sleazy one-night stands with virtue. (Picture Eddie Haskell from *Leave It to Beaver*.)

But it is Danny who is standing right in front of me waiting for me to run out of steam, not some ill-dressed mannequin or television character. I'm certain that he knows what his mother and I expect of him, just as I always knew what my parents expected of me. (The first time that I yelled something at my kids that my mother had yelled at me, I knew that I had heard everything she ever said to me that I apparently didn't listen to.)

Peering under the brim of the dirty cap, I can see the whites of Danny's eyes. I *have* been there in South Catatonia. I know that all he wants out of life at this moment is to get out of the house and see his girlfriend Liz. Nothing else matters. It's perhaps not a transcendent ideal, and it won't get him into college, but it is the most real thing in the world to him right now. And if he does the dishes like he is supposed to do on Friday nights, he might actually get to see her.

And there it is: a parent's leverage. Forget all the sage advice, I tell myself. Kids do as they're told to do if there are undesirable consequences as a result of not doing it. That's it. Make sure he takes care of his obligations—like his homework—and then just let him make his own way. He really has heard it all before.

When I pause, he lifts his head just barely to see if I'm through with the lecture. And in the smirk that we instantly share, I can see my little boy behind the stubble and the pimples and the sneer, the one who drew a picture of a big Indian and a little one side by side with the caption "Like Father Like Son." He was a very good boy; he'll be a very good man.

In the meantime, all he wants and needs is for me and his mother to stand behind him while he makes his own mistakes. Which he is apparently determined to make. That's why Harry Truman, who may have been the most unpolitical politician in our century, was right. Find out what children want and advise them to do it.

Their hearts are in the right place. Always. How can they ever be anyplace else?

Benevolence:
Goodness without Goodies

Benevolence is the characteristic element of human-
ity, and the great exercise of it is in loving relatives.
—Tze-Sze,
The Doctrine of the Mean

Benevolence is one of those slippery concepts that
eludes most adults, but is easily grasped by the
sticky fingers and minds of small children.

I'm thinking right here of the scene in *Jane Eyre*
where poor, honest, homely Jane is told by the
wicked Reverend Brocklehurst about the good
little boy who would rather learn a verse of a
Psalm than receive a treat to eat—and then gets
two treats for being so good. Unlike the Reverend, Jane wasn't the least bit fooled. She knew
that being good in order to snag a reward is not
goodness.

Which, again, reminds me of Eddie Haskell,
Wally Cleaver's butt-kissing friend. Phony as a
crisp three-dollar bill, Eddie demonstrated the fine

art of looking benevolent for millions of *Leave It to Beaver* fans in the TV'ed fifties. As long as he thought there was some profit to be made by pretending to be moral or polite or innocent, he could act as angelic as most naive parents fool themselves into believing their own sainted children really are—underneath their unbathed skins. Of course, June and Ward bought his act every time. And, of course, Beaver and every kid watching the show with an IQ over 21 knew that Eddie was a slimy creep.

Which brings me to the *real* nature of benevolence in a real family: Goodness (as a form of benevolence) is little more than the intent—turned to action—to protect someone in the clan from the ordinary human pain that burns within each of us—and sometimes catches fire all around us. Regardless of our most fervent personal desires, we try to protect each other from each other—and ourselves.

Mention the word *benevolence* in my house, and I immediately conjure up the vision of Bay standing rigid in the middle of the basement playroom, fists at his side, smoke curling from his reddened ears, and lips twisted over glistening teeth as he *grells* (a mesolithic combination growl and yell), "ELIZABETH! STOP IT!!!"

Akin to the snarling warning that mother dogs give to their insatiably rooting puppies before a paw swats them away, please understand that it is a wholly *benevolent* grell. However, strip away Bay's inherently benevolent soul, and it is equally clear that all the little boy wanted to do was to deliver a roundhouse of Tysonic proportions to his little sister, who had been nudging and nagging and bugging and smugging him all the way to the edge of Cain's worst nightmare. He burned to launch her out of the basement window, across the yard, over the trees, and forever out of his limited sight.

But he didn't. Instead of clocking his little sister, Bay grelled. And he grelled loud. He grelled nasty. He grelled like a rampaging dinosaur in a Japanese monster movie. But he did not lift his shaking fists from his rigid sides. He did not throw the Sega controller at his feet. He did not knock her down with a monstrous shove.

With every fiber of his being urging him to wipe that twinky little smirk off his sister's face, he did the kindest thing he could do—given his age and the shortness of his burning fuse. He knew in his soul that it would be wrong—and most unkind—to clock her. So he clenched his fists; he twisted his mouth; he grelled like Rodan. It was probably the most loving grell I've heard in all my years of parenting. And that is finally the heart of true benevolence.

So, benevolence is Bay not hitting Elizabeth.

And benevolence is Elizabeth stealing into my bedroom while I'm down with the flu, against her mother's direct warnings to "Leave Daddy alone!" I am, like most dads, a deplorable child when I get sick. I'm not only ornery and contagious and unshaven and most undaddy-like, but I feel utterly alone and abandoned by friends and family, who apparently have no interest in spending time with a seedy, infectious, overgrown seven-year-old. In short, I am pathetic. And there suddenly stands brave little Elizabeth like an angelic vision at the foot of the bed—bucking both invisible viruses and the admonitions of her powerful mama—asking me in that sweet, lisping, unreproducible voice if I'm feeling any better.

Well, I am definitely not feeling any better, but as soon as I look over at that vision of goodness, I feel obligated to I say that I am, I am. I am. I truly am. And such is benevolence.

Benevolence is also Danny—suddenly embarrassed, irked, claustrophobic, and frightened by the sight of his mother walking into the high school cafeteria—not ducking out of the room or sliding under the table or pretending that Patti is an unrecognizable, faceless head of lettuce who bears no relationship to him at all.

Benevolence is Clover telling Addie that her brand-new white swimsuit becomes instantly see-through when it is wet—instead of lying and enjoying the sight of her big sister parading around the gawking pool like a clueless empress in her brand-new clothes.

Benevolence is Addie, who on occasion lets Danny drive her beloved Jeep. Despite the fact that she is utterly convinced that he—or anybody else in the family, for that matter—is fully capable of wrapping the Wrangler around a tree in order to pay her back for real and imagined insults, she knows the machine is a "chick magnet." (Dan thinks he's the magnet.)

Benevolence is Nancy, who has finally forgiven me for taking thirty-six posed and choreographed snapshots of her junior prom with an empty camera. (Yes, sadly, it is true. Mea culpa. Mea culpa. Mea culpa.) In some families, the legal fees associated with a capital trial, not to mention the cost of psycho- and/or physical therapy after such a gaffe, would lead to seven generations of unrelenting moral and financial bankruptcy.

Benevolence is Cael, who recently had to walk out of a club in Chapel Hill before he went chin to chin with some guy who was merely trying to talk to (and, of course, charm) his little sister Clover.

Benevolence is Patti, a distinctly alluring woman who gracefully turns away from ordinary flirtatious fun—in the form of handsome front-door suitors, manly back-door roosters, and shady men of all shapes and sizes—which allows me to understand that while I don't deserve her love, it is entirely mine without even asking.

And, finally, benevolence is me for not writing down all the hideously embarrassing stories I could tell about my perfectly imperfect family, driving them to murderous distraction, just like Elizabeth likes to do to Bay. Smirk. Smirk.

Babying Babies:
Why It's Impossible to Spoil an Infant

> Infancy conforms to nobody; all conform to it.
> —Ralph Waldo Emerson,
> *Self-Reliance*

You're in that deliciously warm and powdery atmosphere, leaning over the edge of a white crib, peering down at that sweet-smelling bundle of soft DNA and fuzzy protoplasm. You flash a smile as big as a big-screen TV at those dark, dark marbles of eyes fixed in Zenlike emptiness on your awe-enraptured face. You coo, you warble, you snicker, you snort, you make some rather undignified high-pitched repetitive birdlike peeps, hoping beyond even unreasonable reason to make soulful and intelligent contact with that redemptive bundle of wonder on the bunny-and-chick fitted sheet.

But the toothless darkness behind the tiny circle of mouth does not answer. A twitch here. A gaseous smile there. An arm flung up and dropped. And pretty soon you find yourself fixated on that cute but annoying little tab of skin on her upper lip, wondering if there is anything at all going on inside that enormous little head. Anything?

Well, if you'll tiptoe out of the nursery with me, I'll share some of my confusion on the subject.

After leaning for hours upon years over the cribs of seven well-powdered infants who offered similarly blank stares during their first few days of life, I have to admit that I never received one message to suggest that there is anything remotely resembling a conscious thought in my babies' heads. Yes, the elevator goes up there, the lights go on and off, and judging by the fatness of the bellies, there's food in the fridge. But the doorbell doesn't ring. If you're not her mother, she doesn't even know you're there.

While I'm certain that each baby has a distinct personality at birth, I'm equally convinced that the little cherub with fluttering wings hasn't quite landed on both feet in that bulbous skull as of yet. And although I know at my core that every newborn has a soul that is immutable (how can I not be me?), I also have come to realize that the soft, beautiful, pure essence in the crib experiences little more than cosmic pleasure and haunting pain.

Which is why anyone who contends that you will spoil a baby by feeding her on demand or holding him whenever he cries is not only wrong, but frightfully ridiculous. Babies cry simply because they are hungry or uncomfortable or scared. If we don't pick them up immediately, the only thing they experience is more hunger, more discomfort, more fear—and they are less likely to be trusting when they finally do have a thought in their heads.

Too many politicians and social theorists with political agendas love to point at Doc Spock as the perpetrator of the ever-present generation of spoiled brats, all because back in the fifties he suggested that babies should be fed when they're hungry, not on a schedule. Based on the presumption that newborns are manipulative little imps whose sole intent in wailing is to exercise arbitrary power over the very people who are necessary to their survival, the vigilant voices behind those pointing fingers cheerfully advise moms and dads that if they give in to children when they're babies, they're going to own you when they get to be teenagers.

But here is a real family value: *Everyone in the family should be a loving and devoted servant to the baby during those first few months of life.* Everyone, especially the parents, should attend to the infant's every need as soon as it is heard. And everyone, particularly the baby, should know that there is nothing more important than making that baby feel safe and loved. If you want to raise a newborn who is to feel safe and loved—and what could possibly be more important to the moral development of any child?—she should be worn, held, cuddled, talked to, rocked, fed every waking minute of the day that you can stand her scintillating company and are not going to the bathroom. And if you can possibly survive it without losing your REM-sanity, the baby should sleep in your room for at least the first few months of life on this earth. After nine months tucked in and floating inside a mother's temperature-controlled womb with all its accompanying whooshing and gurgling and warbling to keep him company twenty-four hours a day, it must be a soul-shattering shock to be alone in a dark and empty cavern all by yourself, particularly if you don't even know who you are.

I think that one of the reasons so many contemporary children seemingly have little ability to defer immediate gratification may be that they weren't taught—in their cells and in their bones and in their cribs—that their most basic fears would never come to pass. Never allowed to feel absolutely secure that someone would always be there, they have trouble later on distinguishing between a real need—like food or love—and manufactured needs like Cocoa Crispies, cigarettes, Ivy League degrees, corner offices, and BMWs they can't afford.

That's why I was thankful, but not totally astonished, years ago when twelve-year-old Nancy slipped as she carried her infant brother Bay and bounced rather unmerrily all the way down the basement steps to the cement floor below. Thirteen bumps on her pre-adolescent bottom without dropping her hands to break her fall. It must have hurt like hell; she wailed as if she had been deserted by God. But she knew in her heart that if she let him go, he would fly off and be hurt. She knew that it was better that she be hurt than the baby. She knew in her prepubescent soul that we simply can't let go of our infants for even a second in this swirling world. They just fly off. Patti and I never told her that, she just knew it, I suppose because we never let her go.

The process of raising children, it often seems to Patti and me, is one of gradually loosening your grip on your kids' lives until each one is finally ready to leave your loving protection. Whenever that is. Everyone is different. As a rule, though, babies need you all the time; toddlers need you most of the time; elementary school children need you after school; high school children need you at dinner and at curfew; college children simply need a monthly check and someone to answer the phone on Sunday nights. After that, when they no longer belong in their childhood beds, you're needed to somehow let them know it's okay to be off on their own. (And that you'll be around when they can't stand being around their own kids.)

Charity:
Bringin' It All Back Home

> Charity and personal force are the only investments worth anything.
>
> —Walt Whitman,
> "Song of Prudence"

Everybody knows that charity begins at home. It emanates from the core of the family and radiates out to warm those closest to the light. And those who are touched by the light, in turn, reflect the warmth toward others who are closest to them.

However, back in 1988 during the presidential campaign, I was so touched by George Bush's ringing vision of charity as "a thousand points of light" that I momentarily forgot about keeping it close to home. The moment I first heard that sound bite, I began to envision each of my family's meager charitable contributions as single rays in a massive beacon that would shed the light of truth and compassion on the most heartrending sides of human misery. The bigger the organization, it seemed, the more needy people could be helped, and the more effective my wrinkled dollar would be in alleviating the world's great pain. I would be a pure, faceless giver among thousands—even millions—of other bright givers, who in supporting national or international charities would reflect the light of selfless giving. I glowed with goodwill.

In fact, I must have glowed ever brighter and brighter with each check I wrote that year, because not long after Mr. Bush took office, I began to feel like a porch light on a humid summer night attracting countless thousands of organizational moths and other flying creatures anxious for my warm beneficence. Slick solicitations—by mail and by phone—came swarming in from big charities all over the globe. They soon became as commonplace as the Victoria's Secret catalogues that I would find almost daily in my battered rural mailbox.

The glut of paper was appalling; the telephone intrusions most aggravating; but the worst was the slow burning realization that the humanitarian alliances that Patti and I supported—the "good guys" who would work to save the environment, feed the hungry, rescue the Constitution, and protect human dignity—had begun to pursue my dollar as if they were on the marketing staffs of Fortune 500 companies. They might as well have been promoting deodorant tampons or aluminum siding as promising to feed the hungry Sri Lankans. I began to feel most uncharitable.

At that time in my family's busy life (Cael and Nancy in college, Addie and Clover in high school, Danny in middle school, Bay in elementary school, Elizabeth in nursery school), there were two absolutely predictable events that would occur like clockwork the moment we sat down to dinner. First, Clover's best friend, Jessica Chapman, would call. (I remain convinced all these years later that Jessica had secretly installed a device that would alert her to the precise moment that the oven was turned off.) And then shortly after Jessica was told that Clover was eating dinner, the phone would ring again with a solicitation from an aluminum siding business or a credit card company or, in increasing uncharitable frequency, a big-time charity. Jessica was always welcome; the solicitors, never.

And thus, on March 15, 1992, moments after once again telling Jessica that Clover would call her back after dinner, I went into my full barbaric yawp, right in the unsuspecting ear of some well-intentioned volunteer from an environmental group (I had previously supported) whose job it was to try to separate me from my money as I was sitting down to eat with my family, that is, when I was relaxed and letting go of the cares of the world. I muttered *"Et tu, Brute,"* but he didn't get it. I crowed on about intrusions, about phony "special appeals," about sleazy name exchange with other organizations, about renewal notices six months ahead of schedule, about silly magazines . . . about all the issues that would fit neatly into the phrase "ruin my appetite."

The voice in lieu of a young man was clueless. He apologized and asked if I wanted him to call back at a better time.

"Noooooooooo!!" I howled and hung up.

I felt sorry for him, but I'd had enough of charitable mendacity, as Big Daddy might have said. The keepers of the big lights may indeed assure themselves that their petty dishonesties serve good causes, that they do only what is necessary to achieve their worthy goals, and that good people like you and me should wise up—and ante up. But that evening, I understood that it's just the same old pitch in a new and improved package: create an itch that the ignorant—and guilt-ridden—consumers feel compelled to scratch with checks they cannot easily afford to write.

Returning to the dinner table, I vowed to unscrew myself from The Big Star, leaving one tiny dark socket in the national marquee. I took my sixty watts back here to the Hudson Valley where I live, where I breathe, where I work, where I rub elbows with neighbors, where we shed the light of truth on each other day after day after working day. Where the pain and suffering are right off my front porch, every bit as real as they are thousands of miles away.

Between the salad and the potatoes (and the spilled water)

that evening, I realized that charity is not necessarily big or even overwhelmingly bright. It is simply the compassionate act of one person giving a hand to another person who has fallen along the same dark, potholed, winding toll road we all seem to travel together. A personal force. The neighborly thing to do. A light: sometimes a road flare, sometimes a penlight, sometimes a flickering candle that allows us to see the face of need. A humbling reminder that *There but for the grace of God go I.*

That night at dinner I effectively closed the ledger on all enterprises east of Millerton, north of Tivoli, west of the Minnewaska Ridge, south of the Newburgh–Beacon Bridge. For the first time, I think I really understood being thankful for the bread that was on my table.

The warm glow from my checkbook now goes exclusively toward helping to light up the local rescue squad, the fire department, booster groups, county families in need, the homeless, the regional land trust, the town recycling project, the class of '97, the Little League. Charities that enable me to see how much I am needed, not how good I am. (Of course, my revelation didn't alter Jessica's calling schedule, but I did feel increasingly charitable about the interruptions—and, frankly, quite sad when the two best friends grew up and the phone stopped ringing at dinner.)

Loving Chaos:
The Order of an Ordinary Family Day

> Accidents will happen, even in the best regulated families.
>
> —Charles Dickens,
> *David Copperfield*

One of the virtues of having seven children is that in order to remain relatively sane, Patti and I have found it necessary to give up the All-American illusion of maintaining a house that is clean and orderly at the same time. Clean is good for obvious reasons. Orderly is impossible without grave psychospiritual penalties.

With one or two kids in the house, many parents may be inclined to think that they are in control of the daily workings of the family, but as one who has stumbled over that particular cliff five times, I know that household control is a wishful hallucination. The very moment that child #3 enters the world and upsets the precarious symmetry of family photo opportunities (2 parents, 2 children—1 boy, 1 girl—2 cars, a dog, and a cat) and the kids suddenly outnumber the parents, the thin if wholesome myth of order shatters like a tall glass of milk falling off the edge of the kitchen table.

In a sense, the dizzying fall that inevitably follows the realization is beyond your grasp. It reminds me of those trust exercises that drama students and group therapy participants love so well: falling straight backwards into the collective arms of your comrades—or your family, in this case. If you're going to have kids, you have to just drop. Buckle your knees to break the fall and you'll risk wrenching your lower back; twist your head to see the future and you might break your neck; flap your hands backward to regain your precarious balance and you'll get tangled in the mesh of arms that are meant to catch you, falling hard and fast between the cracks. You must trust that the ground will not be pure hard floor but cushioned by the accumulated debris of daily life.

Many regular families with one or two kids—a state of mind that we visited briefly between July 1969 and December 1974—are victims of the hoax that politicians and former Junior Leaguers past childbearing age have been foisting on the childish public since the childless George Washington tricked us all into calling him the Father of Our Country: that with the proper planning, good taste, the will to see one's visions come to completion, a pure heart, an orderly mind, and faith in God and country, anything and everything can be accomplished on time, without tears, without screaming, and without breaking into a cold sweat. Civilized Meals, for example. An Immaculately Clean House, for another. Well-Planned Family Vacations, for one more. And as long as I'm dreaming, A Roll of Toilet Paper Always on the Toilet Paper Holder. In all, perfect domestic harmony. A Disney-choreographed White House Christmas. A Martha Stewart Stepford Family picnic.

Give it up.

If you watch too much television or heed the disingenuous advice of too many public figures prattling on about cleanliness and godliness, order would seem to be a family value. It is not.

Disorder is the order of the day in any normal family. Just look around. In my house everything moves toward disintegration: plates drop, socks are mysteriously lost in the wash, buttons fall off, zippers snag, tights run, the kitchen table rocks unstably, the living room couch sinks, nails loosen in the sheetrock. Everything and everybody resists control: feet keep growing, the lawn is overrun with crabgrass, dust miraculously appears out of nowhere and settles in the newly vacuumed living room, lewd thoughts enter the pure minds of little boys and girls, hair frizzes, the remote control disappears, tempers flare. Flu happens. I know it's hard to believe, but I have discovered that children sometimes do not do as they're told. And nothing ever works exactly as it is supposed to work.

I'm not suggesting that anyone abandon the quest for family order. Rules and traditions and notions of efficiency help to keep us from the despair that chaos creates in its wake. And if cleanliness is not really next to godliness, it's right up there with good health and citizenship.

But aspiring to a clean house or a neat and tidy garage (or playroom or yard or basement) is remarkably different from actually keeping a picture-perfect family life—or demanding that of your hapless family. The latter demands perfection of patently imperfect beings, and you're defeated before you even begin. The floors will never be shiny enough; the woodwork will never be white enough; the corner of the rug will turn up and taunt you; the spiders in the corners of the most immaculate rooms will inscribe your name in their webs; your children will never be cute enough, well behaved enough, quiet enough, smart enough, entertained enough, grateful enough. You will squander your life cleaning up and planning for the big party that will be held directly after your funeral.

In contrast, once you understand that a house that looks lived in is actually lived in, you might actually walk into the living room and not be afraid of knocking anything over. You might slump down into the couch unconcerned about the perfectly fluffed pillows. You might take your shoes off and put your aching feet up on the coffee table and say, "Ahhhhh." You might even relax in the knowledge that when you're refreshed (or company is arriving), the dishes will get washed, the gutters cleaned, the floors mopped, the mounting laundry attacked.

Danny's bedroom provides an enduring vision for this family value. So profoundly disheveled is his private space—clothes and towels covering every inch of floor, bed unmade, closet door off its hinges, a cracked window where he misthrew a dart, a desk hidden underneath piles of newspapers, notebooks, tissues, shinguards, and things I can't identify and don't want to touch for fear that I will spawn a modern-day Black Plague. The smell in there is almost otherworldly: a mix of Drakar, mildew, testosterone, his best friends Sheck and Sammons, and sheets that may not have been changed in months.

Patti actually demands a reordering of the mess on a weekly basis—lips taut, index finger pointed at a weekend grounding—and I agree with her. If nothing else, he should guard against disease (and, along the way, learn the value of valuing your own space on this earth).

But I have also come to see Danny's room as a work of art to be appreciated. It's an expression of the utter chaos that covers and cushions the overly regulated life of an ordinary seventeen-year-old whose days are overwrought with expectations from parents, teachers, bosses, and coaches for complete acquiescence to adult ideals. He looks around his messy room and knows that if nothing else, there is something in the world over which he has dominion.

And I know that later on, when Danny confronts the real chaos of adult existence, he'll probably want a neat house. He'll appreciate a coat hung up, a drawer closed. So when the sight of his room offends my sense of decency, I simply close the door and move on up the stairs to my eternally messy study, postcards and ticket stubs tacked to the walls, books stacked precariously in tilting bookshelves, coffee cups on the windowsill. It's mine.

Discipline:
Holding the Line Against Forty-Seven-Pound Elizabeth

> There is little less trouble in governing a private family than a whole kingdom.
> —Michel de Montaigne,
> *Essays*

Elizabeth is part angel, with a sweet heart, a floppy mop of brown pigtails, and an absurd enthusiasm for the mundane. Yet she's also part imp, with a wicked smirk, a dirty smudge on her cheek, and dark fathomless eyes that could make a grown man quiver.

Which is what I was doing one Saturday morning after telling her that she wasn't allowed to have her best friend, Kathleen (pronounced Kaf-uh-ween), over in the afternoon because she hadn't cleaned up the domestic landfill that doubles as the basement playroom. She instinctively looked around my hip to see if her mother agreed, but as Patti was away on a trip with Clover, there was no higher authority to whom she could fashion an appeal. That's when she summoned up THE GLANCE—eyebrows aslant, lips pressed together in a scowl, nostrils flaring—that pushed me right up to the edge of a parent's worst trap: letting on that you're afraid of your kid.

The truth is that she deserved her mild punishment. I knew that. She knew that. There was no need for me to be quaking like a little kid going nose to nose with the neighborhood bully. But, like many parents, I hate to punish my kids. My knee-jerk response to everything they do is to try to smooth things out. For me the cold shoulder of a child is a chilling fate worse than death. At heart, I'm a wimp.

So the easy thing would have been to let it slide and allow Kathleen to come over—especially with Friday's unfinished work, bills to pay, a trip to the dump, carpooling and mowing complicating the "day off" ahead of me. But as I have come to understand in the process of raising our seven uncivilized angels, children will drive you plate-throwing insane if you don't give them the limits that they want and need.

So I girded up all my latent wimpishness, raked it into a giant lawn and leaf bag, and stood my ground. And when the miniature Hydra asked the whiny "But whyyyy?" I rejected a disastrous impulse to attempt a more reasoned explanation and pointed calmly to the landfill. And when she demanded with teary eyes a better reason than the obvious mess on the floor, I finally understood that my youngest child was, in her own way, giving me a refresher lesson in the *Care and Maintenance of the Domestic Eight-Year-Old.* I uttered the politically unfashionable "Because I say so."

That she understood, instantly wailing out how mean and cruel I was and how she wished her mommy was around. I agreed. And when she turned a very cold shoulder on me and started picking up the first of a half-ton of toys, I was practically devastated. But still standing.

It's not easy. Certainly not as effortless as it sounds in those parenting magazines in your bathroom—or the books on discipline piled on your bedside table. Did you ever notice how they read like popularized business management texts and always seem to have catchy little titles with numbers in them like *3 Easy Ways to Get Your Child to Listen to You* or *The 5-Minute Child Manager* or *7 Days to Complete Domestic Tranquility*? And each one offers the same message-myth that has plagued recent generations of ordinary families: that children can be managed the way bosses manage employees or stockbrokers manage money market funds, that happiness is achieved through organization and consistency.

Of course, with time to think about it, any ordinarily harried parent with a job and a pulse would realize that most bosses don't manage their employees very well, that stockbrokers lose more money than they gain, and that organization and consistency are the most elusive of family values.

My good friend Pete Wilkinson, a captain in the Town of Poughkeepsie Police Department, expresses the problem rather poignantly: "All day long I give orders to dozens of people and every one of them listens to me. Usually right away. Then I come home and see a little something that needs to be done around the house and all I do is tell my kids Nicolle and Cody to take care of it, and they look at me as if I've just stepped off the starship *Enterprise* and they don't recognize my authority in their solar system. It's very confusing."

I agree. Patti and I have been raising babies since the original Woodstock—and are still trying to keep the music playing and the toys on the shelves and the plates on the table as Bay and Elizabeth Bayou-Grace have followed the trail of scowling looks and dirty laundry left by Danny, Clover, Addie, Nancy, and Cael. And although the terms *discipline* and *problems* seem to fit together as naturally as peanut butter and jelly these days, we try to start each day under the premise that discipline problems are a normal and expected function of raising strong, healthy, well-mannered, and assertive children. Kids need to challenge the boundaries at home. And parents need to stand their rightful ground. If not, how will our children learn when to stand up against bosses, lovers, children, and their own innate wimpishness—and when to sit down?

The only thing that seems to matter is keeping a clear perspective on who is actually pretending to be the parent and who is best suited to be the child. The politically incorrect phrase from my childhood, *Because I say so*—which is sometimes confused with the more childlike *Because*—is a staple in our parental lexicon, not because we love power over urchins, but because we've learned that it's exactly the answer that our children want to hear. They long to know that Patti and I won't wimp out on them when it really matters. We know—and they know—just how lost they'd be without us.

Debt:
The Price of Family Togetherness

> It is hard to pay for bread that has already been eaten.
>
> —Danish proverb

After dropping more than thirty bucks at the Mobil Station in New Paltz, Danny, his good friend Jessie, and I were off on a man-sized college road trip. Pedal to the metal on the New York State Thruway. The Black Crows crackling through the broken speakers. Snickers. Tolls. Barbeque chips. Sprites. Burpin'. Reese's. Jock talk. Snapples. Apples. Java. Fast food.

After one bite of the "BLT Taco Special" at a Taco Bell in Towson, Maryland, I knew I had made a bad choice for a digestive system nearly five decades old. But I ate it anyway. After all, I had paid good money for the limp and chewy wad of dough, mayonnaise, and undercooked bacon. And by the time we got back in the car and my stomach started to sway to the tune of "Swing Low, Sweet

Chari-ah-ah-ah-ah-ah-aht," I knew I was going to pay dearly for my indulgence.

Family Economic Principle #1: Parents who abandon their well-considered budgets and routines to go on road trips with their teenagers will foot the bill every day in every way for months to come.

The next day, when we woke up early to visit Jefferson's academic village at the University of Virginia, I could still taste the taco. Even the greasy burgers and fries we scarfed at the College Inn didn't erase the interest on that bacon. However, they did add a certain charming surcharge of their own, which was compounded immediately upon paying the bill. I peered inside my worn leather wallet and blanched. I was sure I was missing at least fifty bucks. Maybe a hundred.

Family Economic Principle #2: Small bills (ones, fives, tens) get sucked out of a wallet more rapidly than BLT tacos wage war on one's digestive system.

Amazingly, after buying some UVA logo nonsense for Bay and Elizabeth back home, I only had $27 left of the crisp, fat wad I had started with. The story of my life.

No matter. I quickly picked myself off the sidewalk and dowsed the main drag for an ATM machine flowing with easy capital. "I'm not sure how I survived without ATM machines," I snorted over to the boys. Unfortunately, I would find an answer to my question right away: the machine flashed an unapologetic note on the screen that there were insufficient funds to complete the transaction. I swore up and down that I had just made a deposit, but the damn insolent machine wouldn't hear of it. And the boys just turned away.

"No big deal," I called out after them. "I still got my plastic friends safe and sound back here." I patted my rear pocket. They were so impressed that they forgot to turn around.

Before we barreled down Route 29 toward the state line to do the college tour thing at the University of North Carolina—and visit Clover, Nancy, Cael, and his fiancée, Melissa—I made a calling card call to Nancy to say that we'd be in around four in the afternoon. She'd round up everybody and then we'd all go out to eat. "Real food," I said, adding magnanimously that she should ask her roommate, Whitney, if she'd like to join us. I didn't have to say that, though.

Family Economic Principle #3: When parents show up at a kid's college, they're obliged to take their friends out for dinner. It's the law.

By the time we hit Chapel Hill, I had $6.73 to my name and I didn't think I had bought anything but a Coke and a Hershey bar. We stopped at the Carolina Pride Shop on Franklin Street before going to Clover's dorm to pick up some more unnecessary presents. Of course, I had to put it all on the credit card.

Nancy showed up at the dorm alone, but Clover wanted to take two friends, Mary and Erin. At this point, it simply didn't matter that I had no cash—and apparently no reserves. I was just pleased to be with the kids in Chapel Hill, to meet Clover's new friends, to dream about being in college again, and to be free of mortgages and bills and loans and interest payments for a few days. And, of course, to be on the road again. Besides, I did have my plastic pals.

From there we all went to Cael's house, where his two roommates, Scott and Kevin, were draped around the living room like starving Dali cows. They said they'd love to join us. Cael suggested someplace I never heard of. I shrugged, and the eleven of us rode off in three cars to a nice-looking restaurant just outside Chapel Hill.

We were led to a long table, sat down, and everyone ordered beers and sodas. Frankly, I was in Father Heaven, taking my kids and their friends out for dinner like some kind of Big Daddy Warbucks, enjoying their beautiful young faces, laughing at their good jokes, opening the menu to find something good and juicy and full of all the cholesterol I'm not supposed to eat.

Which was when Danny scanned the entrees and spoke his now famous family words: "Sucks to be Dad."

My eyes skidded over to the right side of the menu. Big bucks. À la carte big bucks, in fact. My heart sank to my ravenous belly, which started a new round of "Swing Low . . ." My face flushed hypoglycemically as I glanced around the quieted table. "Order anything you'd like," I said with a sickly smile, the old BLT taco reminding me once again of my long-term debt.

What else could I say? *You can order an appetizer or a small salad, not both—and three of you can share a soup.* Of course not. I felt for my wallet and said, "Anything you'd like. Enjoy yourselves!"

Family Economic Principle #4: Hey, it's only plastic. And you won't get the bill for a month. Piece of cake.

We had a great time spending money I didn't have, and then I doled out some more of my plastic loot the next morning at the grocery store and at Breugel's Bagels; some more again at lunch at a place called Spanky's; and finally wrote a bad check to Nancy—for some cash for the road—suggesting quietly that she wait three days to deposit it.

Danny, Jessie, and I pulled into New Paltz late Sunday night. I had $2.37 left after paying the New York Thruway toll. I was in debt to Citibank Visa, Fleet Bank Master Card, American Express, and, worst of all, Nancy Lewis, the only one in the family organized enough to keep track of all debts.

Family Economic Principle #5: Like most middle-class American families, we work hard, we pay our taxes and bills approximately on time, and with what's left, we go out to the movies and dinner every so often. But we don't own much of what we call our own.

One bank has the deed on our house, another bank has dibs on the family car, Sears essentially lends us the fridge and the stove, Flannagan's Furniture still has rights to a cushion or two on the couch, and some credit company named GECAF runs the hard drive on the computer I'm working on right now. And, of course, I'm still paying off that men's road trip to Chapel Hill last winter.

But it was definitely worth it. Like it or not, debt has become a real family value. Despite what we hear and read about the shame of the national debt, this country is supported by families like mine and yours who don't have enough disposable income to just take off on a memorable weekend road trip with the boys without interest and monthly installments. It's a small price to pay to enjoy your children so much. And that includes the taco burn.

Empathy:
A Poetic Value Schools Don't Teach

> A man, to be greatly good, must imagine intensely
> and comprehensively; he must put himself in the
> place of another and of many others; the pains and
> pleasures of his species must become his own.
>   —Percy Bysshe Shelley,
>   *A Defence of Poetry*

"Americans hate poetry," *New York Times* columnist Russell Baker once wrote as a simple statement of fact. As far as I know, no one disagreed. (Don't worry, this isn't just about poetry. I'll get around to empathy—and teenagers—in a minute.)

In this culture we view poetry as something beyond the realm of ordinary people. Poets are considered members of strange, exclusionary sects, self-absorbed and condescending, putting one over on us. They just don't make sense. And, frankly, all they write about is depression, distress, disappointment, and death, which comprise just about everything most of us don't want to think about after a hard day of work. In short, we don't like them.

The truth is, though, that we don't like anyone who makes us feel uncomfortable. And short of poets, there is no group quite as discomforting as a pack of teenagers hanging around a street corner or cruising around town on the bald tires of a rusty Monte Carlo—or flopped down on the linoleum floor of the basement. Supposedly rational creatures following a pre-scribed program leading to responsible adulthood, they are a mess of contradictions. They talk too much; they don't talk at all. They're loud and rowdy; they're aloof and moody. They say nobody understands; they don't listen to good advice. We say "Just say no" about all sorts of things; they say "No" except when moving breathlessly close to each other to say "Yes." We tell them to use their heads; they speak ruthlessly from the heart. Just like poets.

Is it any wonder that parents have been complaining about teenagers since Adam and Eve's boys initiated the concept of sibling rivalry for humankind? In a cycle of contempt that goes way back beyond Socrates, who berated youth for its bad man-ners, laziness, disrespect, and contempt for authority and tra-dition, adults have traditionally scorned adolescents.

And thus teenagers, who through the storm of scorn are only made to feel more alone, more impolite, more slackerly, and more and more contemptuous of adults as they ride the hor-mone highway toward adulthood, learn how to scorn their own teenagers. They become hard of heart. They lose a child's natural inclination to empathize with others.

All of which is to say that just at the time when ordinarily self-absorbed teenagers might most need the comfort, perspec-tive, and, yes, lessons on empathy that ordinarily self-absorbed poets offer to their solitary readers, the two rarely meet on equal ground. In most high schools, poems are laid out on yawn-inducing overhead projectors and then tediously dis-sected for rhyme schemes and symbols. Rather than encourag-ing kids to appreciate poems as pure expressions emerging from the heart of the soul, each unruly piece is squeezed unflat-teringly into a learning slot so that it may be part of multiple-choice tests. Which is pretty much how we treat teenagers in high school: shunt them into manageable "cohorts" and move them along. As H. L. Mencken told us, "School days, I believe, are the unhappiest in the whole span of human existence. They are full of dull, unintelligible tasks, new and unpleasant ordinances, brutal violations of common sense and common decency."

Which is some of the reason why teenagers grow into Americans who hate poetry.

Which is why some people have considered me abjectly cruel—and maybe a little bit nuts—for occasionally making my kids memorize bits and pieces of poems that I've thought they should carry around as tools in their chests. I wish they could have seen Clover (who loved childhood) exuberantly calling out the opening stanza of Wallace Stevens's "The Emperor of Ice-Cream" from the top of the dunes on the Outer Banks: "The only emperor is the emperor of ice-cream."

I'm sorry they could not hear Danny (who loves the horizontal life), waist-deep in the Hatteras surf, groaning out Robert Frost's last lines to "Stopping by Woods on a Snowy Evening": "And miles to go before I sleep, / And miles to go before I sleep."

Then they would see that poetry is the language of teenagers. Not simply because it turns out to be fun or funny or nonsensical (or at least preferable to "There once was a man from Nantucket . . ."), but because of all the virtues and values listed in this book, there is probably none more critical to peaceful coexistence in a family—or in the larger family of humankind—than empathy itself. To be able to feel others' deepest feelings virtually ensures that you won't treat them as objects for ridicule, vindictiveness, abuse, scorn—or your own selfish pleasure.

So, although I am always reluctant to prescribe anything to other parents—because I'm certain there are many paths to the same waterfall—I really do believe that any teenager's life would be enhanced by five special poems introduced (not taught) one per year:

For thirteen-year-olds, I like "The Emperor of Ice-Cream" by

Wallace Stevens. It makes almost no sense to them but provides a wonderful phrase about the loss of illusion and wonder outside the gates of childhood.

"One Art," by Elizabeth Bishop, which speaks of the unspeakable pain of losing a love, provides the words for eternally unrequited fourteen-year-olds.

For mean and pimply fifteen-year-olds, "This Is Just to Say," by William Carlos Williams, calls to mind so simply and beautifully the secret and cruel delights of taking something that is not your own. It will help them know they're not so bad.

Robert Bly's "Driving to Town Late to Mail a Letter" reinforces the wonder—and value—of wasting time for naturally slacking sixteen-year-olds.

And Sharon Olds's "Cambridge Elegy," which tells about the death of her boyfriend, will give seventeen-year-olds a vision of how we honor our childhood—and move on.

I don't have a suggestion for eighteen-year-olds. They should be leaving the house to find their own poetry. And empathy.

> It is an ordinary thing
> to be holy.
> We do such extra-
> ordinary things not
> to be.

James Hazard, Milwaukee poet, told us that.

Edyucayshun:
You Could Fill a Book with What Kids Don't Know

Only the educated are free.

—Epictetus,
Discourses

Craig "Scoop" McKinney, editor of the *New Paltz News*, did a heartwarming feature on my daughter Addie when she was a senior in high school. Scoop came to a track meet and interviewed her for nearly an hour. Snapped her smiling picture right there behind the bleachers.

He asked questions that would yield the kind of sublime answers that weekenders and locals alike want to read about in their small-town weeklies: her favorite teacher, her closest friends, her boyfriend, where she's going to college, her glistening future. He wanted her to complain good-naturedly about growing up in a house with seven kids. He wanted her to mist over and thank her parents for their love and support.

Addie was very polite. And, despite her youth,

she was very savvy. She filled in the blanks for the good reporter, and together they created a profile that aspires to read like a 1957 *Look* magazine testament to the All-American Small-Town Girl. And, forgive my unabashed paternal pride, it was mostly true.

Fortunately—or not—Scoop didn't ask her about what books she read in high school. Perhaps he assumed that she read the same ones he was assigned back in the late fifties. You know, the typical high school "canon" that we all suffered through back then: *Beowulf, The Odyssey, Romeo and Juliet, Julius Caesar, Macbeth, Hamlet, A Tale of Two Cities, Gulliver's Travels, Jane Eyre, Pride and Prejudice, Moby Dick, The Scarlet Letter, A Farewell to Arms, The Great Gatsby* . . . and on. And on. And on.

Through four years of high school English (actually five, counting the accelerated year in eighth grade), my daughter Adelyn was assigned just two novels (*Great Expectations* and *Lord of the Flies*) and two plays by Shakespeare (*Romeo and Juliet* and *Julius Caesar*). That's it. That is it. Five years. Some short stories. Some plays. Some poems. She prepared for several debates. She did everything that was asked of her.

And then suddenly she was graduating, ninth in a class of 122. William Faulkner, Kate Chopin, James Baldwin, Eudora Welty, Joseph Conrad, Virginia Woolf, John Updike, Toni Morrison, and Kurt Vonnegut might as well have been the starting lineup for the Mudville Nine instead of novelists her teachers might have introduced her to.

She graduated from high school on June 26, 1993, and the name Desdemona meant nothing to her. Or Ophelia. Or Regan. (Or Lady Brett Ashley. Or Hester Prynne. Or Carol Milford.)

Had Scoop asked Addie what she read in high school, the ink might have run right out of his pen. He probably would have then felt obliged to follow up and ask how it was possible that an honor student missed out on reading great literature. Then he'd have heard that Addie's older sister Nancy (salutatorian, 1991) read only one Shakespeare play in five years of high school English; and that Clover (1995) and Danny (1997) were well on their way to the same empty literary experience.

Then Scoop would have been onto a real scoop. Perhaps he'd have investigated further and turned the journalistic spotlight onto a whole nation that has become so cynical that it has abandoned its literary past. He might even have found that the effect of this cultural ignorance can be seen not just in lower test scores but in the loss of sympathy for others.

And Scoop might have then reported that just as Hawthorne's Hester Prynne wished for her daughter Pearl a grief that would "humanize and make her capable of sympathy," the great works of literature challenge every reader to acknowledge the "human frailty and sorrow" that bind us together as a people. They show us how passionate, dignified, and intelligent—how much like Hester Prynne—one must be to navigate the moral terrain and find compassion.

But that was not Scoop's job, and he knows his job well, which is why the *New Paltz News* sells lots of papers every week. There's enough pain and ignorance in the world already. Nobody needs to read about trouble in places like Grover's Corners.

Frankly, I have no beef with Scoop McKinney. He is, at heart, a good and decent man. Through Addie—and each of the other neatly packaged All-American small-town kids he interviews in these weekly profiles—he only wants his readers to see the gorgeous smile, and to allow us the harmless indulgence that, at least here, all is well. Unfortunately, it is not.

On hundreds of high school podiums across the nation every June, speakers predictably say something about this being the best of times and the worst of times. But the best and the brightest of our graduates often don't know the derivation of that phrase—or why it's so unsettlingly true.

What can parents do to introduce their children to great books when our schools have devalued reading? Frankly, I don't think we should make reading lists for our kids, just like I don't think parents should be their kids' drill sergeants. We're not here to test their cultural literacy or make them more marketable; we are here mostly to protect their souls against testers and marketers of all kinds.

But perhaps we should be making reading lists for ourselves. (I know that sounds unfair, especially since you probably had to read good books back in high school and thought you were all finished with that.) Yet how else are our kids going to learn to value the pursuit of ideas as much as the pursuit of money or fame or abs of steel? Maybe if we had just one good dog-eared book lying around the house for every TV we own—or for every dozen copies of *Self, Sports Illustrated, Marie Claire,* or *People* on the coffee table, or next to the vast video library of classics like *Dumb and Dumber*—our kids would begin to see their lives less as soap operas and more like great novels.

Fidelity:
A Light in the Window

> He wears his faith as but as the fashion of his hat.
> —William Shakespeare,
> *Much Ado about Nothing*

Unlike politicians, professional athletes, actors, and other media darlings who seem to confuse fidelity with fiddling around, most ordinary folks adhere to the notion of faithfulness to a partner as the cornerstone of a good family life. (Not that most ordinary people actually achieve perfect fidelity, but we do insist on it from our partners, extoll its virtues to our children, and, when we fall from grace, wish it desperately upon ourselves.)

And despite Shere Hite's study suggesting that upwards of 60 percent of married folks cheat on their spouses, most of us still wax sentimental at the drop of an eyelid implying that there is only ONE person in the entire universe meant for each of us. (If that were true, I suppose that fidelity would at least be as common as infidelity.)

In the Ten Commandments that God delivered to Moses on Mount Sinai, not "The Ten Commandments of Love" that The Monotones bestowed upon American teenagers in the early Sixties, fidelity ("Thou shalt not commit adultery") ranks number seven. It comes just after "Thou shalt not kill" and right before "Thou shalt not steal," though we seem to take those two far more seriously than we do the one about fidelity.

Part of the problem, I think, is that the admonitions against murder and robbery are pretty self-explanatory. Nobody wishes either of them upon themselves. Adultery, on the other hand, just seems wrong; and in fact a lot of people do indeed wish it upon themselves.

Of course, you don't need a biblical education to know that if we were all true to our beloveds, there would be a great deal less heartache in the world. Everyone wants to love fearlessly and to be loved unconditionally. There is also the biological view of genetic continuity and faithfulness; we don't want to be sharing immortality with anyone else's genes. And I'm certain that there's a xenophobic economic theory associated with keeping the capital at home. And who in the late 1990s is not painfully aware of the bacterial and viral dangers that abound in the heat of the moment? Even the freest spirits among us understand there's no arguing with AIDS.

But in truth, none of those good reasons is the real reason to be true to your beloved.

Nancy, our oldest daughter, explained the whole thing to me nearly seventeen years ago, when she was a brand-new first grader. Of course, at the time she didn't know she was telling me anything special, and I didn't understand the message until years later, when I started thinking why exactly we revere fidelity.

The bell rang at the old Campus School and Nancy, already being the neat and organized person she was to bring to perfection (a genetic aberration, I suppose), took longer than usual clearing her desk and filling her knapsack. As a result, she was late getting out of the classroom, and as she scurried through the open doors and passed dozens of big second and third graders, one sock up, one sock buried in her sneaker, little Nancy watched in silent horror as her bus pulled away from the curb.

From the safe and detached perspective of adulthood, we all know that the shy little girl could have done any number of things to remedy the situation: yank on a teacher's elbow and say she missed the bus; go back inside the school and tearfully ask the secretary to call her parents; fall to the ground in a heap of elbows and knees and wail hysterically until some adult took pity on her and carried her sobbing to the office—or just drove her the four miles to her home.

Any of those solutions would have worked. But my six-year-old didn't choose any of them. No. She panicked and took off on foot, first running after the bus, which quickly turned the corner and dropped out of her limited sight, then chasing the one and only image of safety and comfort she knew in the entire cold, busy, frightening world.

She raced to the corner, made a left on Mohonk Avenue, and scampered down to South Chestnut Street, where she turned right, her little legs carrying her over to Main Street and across the steel bridge over the Wallkill River.

My heart still races as I imagine her jogging down roads she wasn't even allowed to cross, the corn on either side as high as her father's outstretched hands, turning right on Springtown Road and sprinting full stride past Floyd Patterson's place, Mr. Dipple's farm, the S-turn at Humpo Creek, the tracks, the Campbells' snarling dog, waving breathlessly at Ruthie Sierck, and finally making it all the way home to the old brick house on Coffey Lane. Four miles.

When I asked her why she didn't ask a teacher for help, all the tiny voice said was, "I had to get home."

I didn't really understand what she meant at the time; I was just grateful that she was safe, holding her too tightly and too long against my heaving chest. Recently, however, while speaking to a bereft friend whose wife had had an affair, I remembered Nancy's words, *I had to get home.* When the world falls apart, when you are incapable of thinking logically and rationally, when you simply can't find a way through the darkness of your own fear to get the help you need from anyone, anywhere, then all you can do is race home as fast as your legs or your mind can carry you.

And that home has to be there for you. And it has to be for you only. Always and forever, just as The Monotones told us as we danced cheek to cheek. Anything less and you might run right into the arms of a stranger who will steal the life right out from under you.

Forgiveness:
It Takes Faith

> Forgiveness is the answer to the child's dream of a miracle by which what is broken is made whole again, what is soiled is again made clean.
> —Dag Hammarskjöld,
> *Markings*

It sometimes seems as if Addie has had bad knees forever. Every dismount off the balance beam back in middle school was followed by wincing agonies. Every high school soccer game was defined by how much ice was needed to reduce the swelling. Driving long distances to and from college made her knees stiff and sore.

Patti and I assumed that it all started years before with a minor injury that was aggravated by our headstrong little girl, who refused to rest and let it heal. Several doctors concurred. When she was a sophomore in high school, we took her for arthroscopic surgery on her left knee. It didn't work. When she was a senior, we tried another surgeon for another arthroscopic procedure on her right knee. That operation only added to her pain.

So Addie went off to Penn State with two aching knees and a head full of Chagallian dreams of miracles floating over her pretty head—and a smile that would make it all possible. She had a fabulous freshman year in the storybook town of State College, full of dorm friends and frat parties and football games and classes that truly invigorated her. Yet month by month, her knees seemed to grow more painful. At Christmas, she said she always felt tired. We chalked it up to finals. At Easter, she said she felt old. We teased her about not being eighteen anymore. Of course. She was just nineteen, as invincible as when she was two years old and we called her the Bulldozer.

That summer, with another doctor making even less sense than the ones before, I tacked my Wal-Mart medical diploma to the wall and made the diagnosis that Addie had Lyme disease. After all, we live right in the middle of the woods and dozens of deer graze our yard every day—and Patti, Clover, Nancy, and I had already been treated for the disease—and Lyme can cause joint problems and extreme fatigue. It seemed so obvious. So we had her tested.

As these things go in a universe where well-meaning but essentially clueless human beings—like Dr. Me—sometimes trip down wrong pathways and somehow find right answers, the test came back negative for Lyme. But the doctor told me over the phone with a scratchy voice that Addie had a positive ANA, which he explained is one of the indications of lupus. He advised us to see a rheumatologist right away.

I don't think I ever said good-bye to the well-meaning physician; just hung up the phone short of breath, long on disbelief. At the time, the only other person I "knew" with lupus was the writer Flannery O'Connor. She died of the disease in 1964.

It was a sharp slap across the face for Addie's mother and me, who sometimes think we can protect our kids from anything. And it was a punch in the stomach for our pretty and smart nineteen-year-old, who once figured there was no limit to where she could go with her dreams—who, it seemed to everyone who knew her, was the living embodiment of a Nike commercial.

Lupus is a little-known and less understood autoimmune condition that attacks the joints, the kidneys, and sometimes the central nervous system. Dr. Jill Buyon at the Hospital for Joint Diseases assured us that with all the recent advances in lupus research—and proper medication and monitoring— Addie could very well lead a full and uneventful life. But just as we all inhaled a deep cocktail of relief, the doctor warned us that there were no guarantees that the disease would not progress beyond where it was. The ultimate course of the illness, she acknowledged, was beyond anyone's control—as are all events in our fragile lives. And the possibilities, as she proceeded to lay them out for us, were downright chilling. Even now, with things seemingly under control by way of medication and a remarkably healthy lifestyle, I don't want to drive down that street, not even here on the safe and detached page.

You know the Dr. Seuss book *Oh, the Places You'll Go!* that speakers love to read at high school graduations? Oh, oh, oh . . . the places Addie traveled to after that consciousness-altering visit, so suddenly pushed through the childhood gates, racing down slick highways desperately trying to keep ahead of the tornado behind her, and then skidding into a wall built with the stones of childhood illusions.

In the early days, as she struggled mightily to beat down that unbeatable wall and live her life as if nothing was wrong, Addie volunteered to coach youth soccer on knees that ached before she woke up in the morning; she enrolled in too many courses at college; she partied too hard and too late trying to blot out the sun; and when it rose anyway, she stayed too long on the beach, tempting a systemic crisis. She was angry at Patti and me for passing along the questionable gene. She was furious at Nancy and Clover for their freedom, for their unencumbered futures. She was scornful of Cael, Danny, and Bay for their arrogant, unhealthy ways. She despaired that anything would be right again. She stood on the upper deck of the cottage on Hatteras Island and railed mightily against the injustice in the universe, in the family, in her once perfect body.

And then, somehow, somewhere, for reasons beyond my fatherly understanding, she began to let go of her anger and her pain the way one lets go of a struggling kite on a windy beach, the long string slipping through one's fingers. As I've learned from countless teenagers at home and in the classroom, we do indeed have to lose a child's unwavering trust to gain real faith in the universe.

The following spring she interned at a physical therapy facility and saw how some people allowed their pain to consume them completely, while others moved beyond it. A month later, while Patti and Clover were in Africa—as Elizabeth's "mother" for three weeks—Addie bonded with the one person in the family who truly knows unfairness in her bones. Next, a good friend of hers became a father, and Addie held his child, and she understood how men and women survive the coldest, darkest, loneliest ordeals.

And finally, a few months after her twenty-second birthday, Addie became the first Lewis to enter the prickly realm of body ornamentation. She got a tattoo at a joint called Orleans Ink in the French Quarter of New Orleans. The mark is located in the small of her pinkish back right on the spine. She has to turn around and lift her shirt—and bend the waistband of her jeans—to show it to you. It's a rather pretty drawing of a rune surrounded by green vines. A rune is an ancient Nordic symbol often carved into small rocks for luck or faith. And Addie's rune—which looks like a small *r*—is the symbol for health and strength.

I think it's safe to assume that most tattoo-free parents don't bubble over with joy when a child of any age shows up with body art that doesn't wash off. There's something deep in the parental heart that just makes it seem wrong to place anything permanent or unnatural on those naturally fluid and flawless young bodies, regardless of how pretty or artful or meaningful the picture.

Yet life in real families sometimes alters the chemistry of even the most rigid solutions. And upon seeing Addie's tattoo for the first time, I actually felt a strong surge of health and strength myself, strong enough even to clear the dry constriction in my throat. Not because it was so tastefully done. Not because I was charmed by the rune. Not because it was smaller than I feared. Not even because she seemed so pleased with herself. But only because I knew that Addie had finally forgiven the universe for her pain. And it took all the faith that she had to do it.

Hidden from public view, it is Addie's charmed statement to the world that all is well within her; that she has an enduring faith in the rightness of nature that is unshaken by childhood expectations; that she is not being punished; that, finally, she forgives the gods for her affliction.

And with that she moves along in health and strength to meet her future, as whole and clear and clean as the day she was born. Just like the rest of our kids, who remain tattoo-free, at least for the time being. And at least as far as we know.

G

Generosity:
The Importance of Being Good to Yourself

> Cast thy bread upon the waters; for thou shalt find it after many days.
>
> —*Ecclesiastes* 11:1

I eat what passes for breakfast (a bagel and a cup of coffee) alone in front of the computer screen most mornings. Five or six hours later I generally consume a facsimile of what might be called a healthy lunch (processed turkey on rye, lettuce and mustard, no killer mayonnaise) alone in the car or behind a closed door in my office at Empire State College (computer on, piles of papers buffeting me from the outside world, phone ringing)— or I don't eat at all, stuffing my mouth at low-sugar intervals during those long Sturm und Drang afternoons with a stash of stale reduced-salt pretzels.

I'm not grumbling. I'm also not bragging. If there's one defining complaint heard at the end of the twentieth century, it's that it seems as if no one has time to do anything—especially the things one needs to do. Like sleep. Or eat.

We're just not very generous to ourselves. In fact, I'm sure my *blunch* habits sound familiar to many of you who live life (and eat food) on the run—which is most of you. And this pattern of nutritional abuse is hardly surprising in a culture where many people obtain their Minimum Daily Requirements at McDonald's and where perhaps the most revered and reviled president of the twentieth century, Ronald Reagan, identified ketchup as a vegetable in school lunches.

Which is probably where the ungenerous pattern of grabbing-what-you-can-while-you-can truly begins. At the Duzine Elementary School in New Paltz, for example, the children are allotted all of twenty-two minutes for lunch. That's fine if eating is all the children have to do in those twenty-two minutes; as any parent knows, kids can shovel in a five-course meal, even a nasty school lunch, faster than a dog slurping up a plate of chopped sirloin. Unfortunately, in those twenty-two minutes the kids have to walk—not run—from their classes to the cafeteria; they have to wait in line (sometimes more than fifteen minutes) to get a trayful of what might pass for military grub in *MASH* reruns; find a table with their friends amid the noisy chaos of a hundred other Lilliputian prisoners under the age of eight; manage to get the attention of one of the four harried wardens-cum-aides to help them open the impossible-to-open milk cartons and boxed drinks; eat; throw out the garbage; stash the tray; and then go outside for a twenty-two-minute recess, probably the single most important time slot of the long school day.

Soon after Elizabeth entered kindergarten in September 1993, we noticed that she would arrive home from school with a ravenous appetite. A starving chicken hen with pigtails pecking at anything she could reach in the pantry. She said she was just hungry. We thought otherwise. And utilizing a rather convoluted form of the Socratic method, whereby a clueless parent attempts to wrest information from a young child by assuring her that telling the truth about what goes on at school is not going to land her in the ghoulish principal's office, we found that there were days when, after standing quietly on line and waiting patiently for the cafeteria aide to open up her boxed drink, Elizabeth would manage only a bite or two of lunch before the bell rang.

So when Patti went to the school to observe the problem first-hand, she actually saw some kids—the cute little skinny kindergartners at the back of the line—pick up their trays with only three or four minutes left in the lunch period, walk three steps, dump the entire contents in the garbage (I'm not editorializing here), and follow their racing, screaming friends outside to play for the recess portion of the lunchtime break before returning to their classrooms.

And that would be lunch.

Of course it's a travesty; probably a national travesty, but it seems clear to me that the pace of contemporary life is not about to change anytime soon. And maybe the twenty-two-minute lunch travesty is, after all, an important learning experience for children preparing for life in the twenty-first century. Your mother may have insisted that you chew your food well, and your doctor may warn you about the dangers of clogging your airway, but your teacher, your vice principal, your coach, your boss, and the doleful Congress want you to get back to work before the bell rings. No dawdling. No slackers. Stuff yourself, chew with your mouth open if it's more efficient, wash it all down with anything liquid, just lose it and then get back on task.

Which is the reason sitting down and eating the big meal of the day with the entire family is nearing its obsolesence as we warp-speed toward the millennium. Family dinner is, bottom line, a high-maintenance, low-return, labor-intensive, time-consuming, nonproductive activity that is simply too hard to justify in a market-driven economy. Time is the one commodity that we can't afford to be generous with.

Which is precisely why the traditional gathering around the supper table is too important to abandon. In this, the land of the abundant breakfast bar, practically nothing else in our lives will provide the starchy glue that keeps family members from flying further apart in this fragmented universe.

To do daily family dinners right, you must be generous with your time. It's crucial that everyone in the family actually has to stop what they've been doing all day, come home at a reasonable hour, wash their hands, sit down at a table that is neither desk nor ornamental decoration, put napkins on their laps, pour drinks, cut meat that someone prepared, pass salt, make gossip, foment arguments, spill drinks, discuss arrangements, kick siblings, and laugh until milk comes out of someone's nose.

The rules once everyone is seated are basically the same ones that Adam and Eve laid out for their active boys way back when humankind was just beginning to understand sibling rivalry:

1. Don't lean backwards (you could crack your head open)
2. Use a fork (you're not a chimpanzee)
3. Don't wipe your mouth on your sleeve (what do you think the napkin is there for?)
4. No reading at the table (it's rude)
5. No TV (duh)
6. No leaving the table before everyone is finished (do you think that the meal is made for you alone?)
7. No burping (read the chapter on manners)
8. Clear your place (who do you think you are?)
9. Wash the dishes (it's your turn!)

Otherwise, it's not a family dinner. Otherwise, one day runs right into the next. Otherwise, you think that nourishment comes from saving time, practically the only thing in the universe that you can't save. Otherwise, you might think that food fills the emptiness in your starving soul. Or that food, in the form of power lunches, is merely a suitable lubrication for shoving one person's business down another one's throat.

Otherwise, you're all alone out there every day in a dog-eat-dog world. Be kind. Be generous.

The Golden Rule:
Revisited

> Do not do unto others as you would that they do
> unto you. Their tastes may not be the same.
> —George Bernard Shaw,
> *Man and Superman*

Take a moment and consider the exquisite fairness of the Golden Rule: "All things whatsoever that ye would that men should do to you, do ye even so to them: for this is the law and the prophets" (Matthew 7:12). How can anyone argue with that kind of human and humane logic?

Read it again, this time imagining your mother's voice (without the biblical italics and the stuffy language): "Do to others as you would have them do to you." It seems so true and right, a warm beacon in a sea of selfishness, a gentle enduring reminder of the way human beings at our best might learn to live in harmony. To disagree might be more blasphemous than speaking ill of motherhood or Mother Teresa or Walter Cronkite.

What is right for me is right for you. Right? Wrong.

Unless you're talking about the Ten Commandments, perhaps the only rules in real life not meant to be broken, everything else in real life is relative. Relative to time, age, circumstance, need, desire, yadda yadda yadda yadda. But in daily practice, mostly relative to relatives.

And in my relatively well lived-in house, the banister dulled by millions of applications of palm oil, the grand old rule is about as useless as the sterling silver law about keeping your feet off the coffee table. In the daily comings and goings (some might say rantings and ravings) of a large brood for whom personal identity is sometimes more important than food, assuming that what I want is what you want can be downright perilous to your health. At the risk of exclusion and permanent banishment from Pat Boone's most virtuous inner circle, I'd have to say that George Bernard Shaw's variation on the Rule's goldenness seems closer to what I see just before I turn out the lights each night—and the mafia-inspired bumper sticker is closer still to the worldly ethic I see after I drive out of here each morning: You Toucha My Car, I Breaka Your Face.

In this family, it is an axiom that *there will never be a moment where everyone wants the same thing at the same time.* Food, clothing, music, art, TV, sports, love, affection . . . as Addie says, "What . . . ever." If, for example, Patti cooked only what she would love to eat, Clover would have died in elementary school, Cael would now weigh 450 pounds, and I'd be on my fifteenth coronary bypass. We simply don't have the same tastes—or needs. Or capacity to ingest mayonnaise.

But the recalibration of the golden rule doesn't end in the dining room. Try the living room: I admit to the unfortunate habit of giving my children music that I like. Last Hanukkah I gave Clover a tape by the Violent Femmes. She smiled sweetly and gave me a peck on the cheek, and then pointedly left the thing on the sideboard, where it spent the next nine months gathering wholly ungracious dust. Each day I would see it lying there, still in shrink-wrapped plastic, and I would feel a twinge of pain in my stiffened neck at her lack of gratitude for something I like so much—and that she should treasure as well. (I figured she should at least hide it in her room.)

I eventually got over my selfish insistence that she love what I love—and gave it to a student of mine who does love the Violent Femmes—but since then I still find myself trying to foist my tastes on the family with "gifts" of clothing (that they'll never wear), Chinese takeout dishes (that they never eat), books (that they never read), and posters (that never make a wall). I'm good with jewelry—possibly because I don't wear any—and I know enough not to give someone I like art. But that's it.

Now try the bedroom (no, not that, although that, too): Let's say someone in the family has been dealt a humbling blow by one of life's little instructional events and is lying face down on the bed. And say—just hypothetically—that since I love to be consoled (head on lap, fingers through hair, and ooh that cooing voice), I would naturally think that my wife and children would like the same treatment. I learned early and well that it's downright dangerous to try to wrestle anyone in this family down to my lap for some soothing fatherly strokes: Cael paces and fumes, shrugging off any attempt at consolation with a dangerous elbow; Nancy grows silent, crawling into the shell of herself as if you weren't right there stroking her forehead and cooing that everything's going to be all right (which, of course, brings up the old ingratitude thing). Addie grows stiff, muscles taut, brain fixed on hitting the next person who says things are always for the best; Clover turns away with tears clouding her eyes and says everything's fine before you do, reducing you to begging her to let you comfort her; Danny, the Zen master of passive aggression, actually tries to make you feel guilt for his pain by sitting head down and slump-shouldered right in your face; Elizabeth howls inconsolably; Patti, who says she hates to be "pawed" when she's hurt or worried, hides double-edged razors in your words of consolation that she sends right back at you like a boomerang.

I thank the heavens for Bay, who will crawl into the cave of my arm when life is too hard and let me stroke him to my heart's content. He just won't let me coo, even if I try to bribe him.

That leaves the kitchen, specifically the kitchen counter, over which most of the serious conversation goes on in many houses. It is there where parents and siblings alike, trying to be honorable and righteous, swap tales and offer one another constructive criticism. Of course, each of us rationalizes the seering criticism by invoking the old Golden Rule and saying something like, "I'm only saying this because I love you and I hope that you'd do the same for me when I'm acting like a jerk. No matter how much it hurts."

Right. Despite the thin smile on the face of the person receiving your most honorable gift, the righteous criticism is almost always received with horror and pain, as if the recipient had been slashed by a carefully hidden box cutter. So whenever someone in the family says to me, "Be brutally honest with me, Dad, tell me what you think . . . ," I try to remember Shaw's golden warning and (taking a step or two backwards just to be safe) tell whoever it is exactly what I think she or he wants to hear.

Unless, of course, it's one of those prickly Ten Commandments . . . and then the old Golden Rule gets revisited like a mean old aunt who tells you exactly how she feels.

Humor:
The Meaning of Life

> One would be in less danger / From the wiles of
> the stranger / If one's own kin and kith / Were
> more fun to be with.
>
> —Ogden Nash,
> "Family Court"

I've long wondered why the Buddha is laughing.
What *is* the big cosmic joke Asians seem to get but
leaves us happy-go-lucky Americans clueless?

We never get to see Jesus portrayed as a lighthearted trickster turning tap water into a Beaujo-
lais nouveau. Moses, as far as I know, wasn't
doing stand-up on Mount Sinai. And God Himself, being far too busy with miracles and important wrathful acts like flooding the world, would
never be confused with a being who has the dry
wit of George Burns (except, of course, in Hollywood, which apparently really does exist). But
there on the other side of the world sits the fat
Buddha, an eternal chuckle on his broad face.

I've also wondered whether Buddha knew about Damma.

Patti's grandmother Damma was ninety-four and suffering congestive heart failure when she finally let out the secret of the meaning of life. Over the phone her voice had sounded weak, the gentle mocking edge lost in the daily quest for oxygen and sleep. Having talked (and cajoled and bluffed and charmed and threatened) her way out of several dates with the Eternal Footman in her late eighties and early nineties, there was not a soul on earth who figured she would survive the latest confrontation with merciless fate. Even the cardiologist, who was treating her with the latest in cavalier care and contraindicated drugs, was not hopeful.

Afraid she'd never see her beloved grandmother again, Patti rushed down to Biloxi, Mississippi, to say her final final good-byes. (Admittedly, she had already made this trip several times before, and after each visit the old woman somehow made another miraculous recovery.)

Damma, who in her prime had been as round as the Buddha, was maybe just as tickled as he was by the absolute ridiculousness of existence. She had long white hair piled precariously on top of her head and enormous breasts that ballooned out the entire front of the many floral print dresses she wore each day. (This changed when she had a double mastectomy at ninety-two, about which she later reflected, "If I knew how good it was going to feel, I'd have had 'em removed years ago!")

This time, however, there were no jokes. Damma's inner light was fading. Unable to lie down because of the heart condition and too weak to get up and walk around, she seemed to be quickly losing the spark that had once lit up and sustained Patti's barefoot weekends and summers on the Gulf Coast.

In retrospect, it seems that Damma had been preparing for death for decades. I remember her giving away—or trying to give away—anything and everything in that unbelievably knickknacked and cluttered cottage on Lee Street. Soon after we were married, Patti began receiving weekly packages in the mail: food, flattened flowers picked from her yard, curious knickknacks that the marvelous old woman had collected from her travels (real and imaginary) around the world. Anything she could stuff into a shoebox. And whenever we visited her, we returned to Wisconsin with bulging suitcases full of things we didn't need or want or know what to do with, anything from piles of threadbare linens pulled out from underneath her bed to ornate tarnished candlestick holders snatched off the dusty mantel.

It seemed that Patti and her cousins had become repositories for Damma's fading dreams. It was clear to everyone in the family that the old woman was simply trying to give away all her earthly possessions so she could fly off to heaven a pure spirit.

But Patti, sitting alone at her grandmother's bedside in the overheated and severely cramped senior citizens apartment, wanted something more than the things that cluttered Damma's life. She was ready for Damma's pronouncement, her punchline. Glancing lovingly at the wonderful old woman who had sustained and nourished her and made her laugh through so many of her own childhood trials, she knew that Damma had wisdom. Not the pomp or sagacity of the writers and thinkers whose bon mots end up in dusty places like *Bartlett's Quotations*, but real wisdom born of a long life nearing the end.

And so the adoring granddaughter, who is ordinarily not given to asking such questions, asked her adored grandmother the ultimate query about existence: "What is the meaning of life, Damma?"

And the withered old woman straightened her bent spine, filled her cheeks with color, and looked straight at her devoted grandchild with a resolve that seemed to say that she had been waiting for years—probably decades—for someone with enough sense to finally ask her just that question.

She didn't hesitate, offering no preambles or apologies or stipulations: "Family," she enunciated very clearly, so as to not have to repeat herself, "sense of humor, and . . ." a stirring pause for stage effect, "real estate."

Patti looked into her grandmother's twinkling eyes but saw no guile, just the pure unadulterated truth, like a row of lemons on a slot machine: Family. Sense of humor. And real estate. Of course. Like all good Sphinxes, Damma didn't elaborate. She just leaned back against the upright pillows, eyelids nearly closed, a smirk at the edge of her lips.

Perhaps there was no need to explain. Perhaps it was enough just to chuckle at the absurd rightness of her proclamation. We need family to sustain ourselves, to make us know that we are never alone; we need a sense of humor to understand that there is nothing personal in the harsh winds that blow down our carefully constructed lives; and we need real estate because it never hurts to have some assets—or roots—to pass on to the next generation.

Scott Peck's famous first line, "Life is hard," which I incidentally believe he stole from my Aunt Sylvia's lame dog, Queenie, challenges each of us to figure out a way to deal with an unpredictable and tragic universe. And basically, it seems as if we have three choices available to each of us: sadness, anger, or belly laughter. Personally, I figure it's better to laugh than cry or rage futilely against the cosmos, but everybody's got to find his or her own way.

And so Patti laughed and cried and laughed some more and said good-bye, returning home to her husband and babies to wait for the call that she never wanted to receive.

Of course, the call never came—or at least it waited four or five more years. A big joke. And Damma giggled like a Buddha all the way to ninety-nine.

Humility:
Yes, Lauren, the Red Sea Did Part

> Don't set out to teach theism from your natural history. . . . You spoil both.
> —Ralph Waldo Emerson,
> *Journals*

As I glanced around the suburban synagogue, I felt more humbled than usual. As someone who has been graced with love since birth, I sometimes fool myself into believing that life is a process of refinements and adjustments (and quick snacks) on a long road leading to a pot of gold at the end of the rainbow. But rites of passage such as this one reminded me that we're really just going around in circles.

Very little had changed since I, too, was thirteen and attending a bar mitzvah per week for one of my friends at Wheatley Junior High. The twenty or so seventh graders in the congregation giggled and squirmed through the service. Two men in the aisle ahead, considerably past their adolescence, whispered about business and shared some hard candy. Aunts smiled through their tears. Great-uncles, lips moving faster than the cantor's, chanted to themselves.

My friend Jon, whose own bar mitzvah I had attended thirty-some-odd years before, was the picture of his own proud papa, beaming at his beautiful daughter Lauren entering woman-hood. On either side of me were Jim and Richard, looking for a split second like they had in 1958 when we first met in seventh grade, the boys still alive behind their crow's-footed eyes. In that humble moment, it seemed a miracle to be together again under one roof.

As the rabbi began his sermon about the parting of the Red Sea, I felt myself receding into the comfort of a story that has been my companion since I was younger than my youngest child. From a distance of some light years, though, I heard the soothing author-itative voice mention that the Red Sea did not actually part.

Did not part? I sat up, swept suddenly back into the inescapable present.

No, he said, it did not part. He was talking about archaeo-logical evidence of a "reed bridge" that the enslaved Jews were able to walk over but that sank under the weight of the heavily armored and charioted Egyptians. Wow.

I have no doubt that the rabbi meant well, but at the time I was rendered slack-jawed by the information. I think I would have been fascinated if we were sitting in Archaeology 101 or watching a "National Geographic" special on TV, but within the confines of the synagogue, I suddenly felt robbed of some-thing vital to my otherwise logical and ordered life.

In my somewhat unmagical middle age, with seven children creating more mystery than I am comfortable with, I have come to believe, like Job, that we live in the midst of an incompre-hensible universe, a few flickers from a fire lighting up the cold cave. We snuggle together to keep warm and feel safe and per-haps a little less clueless.

I do understand, however, that there are many good souls around who disagree with that less-than-cosmic view, who feel that everything in the universe has a purpose that human

beings can understand. Wishing to make sense of all phenom-
ena that seem to defy reason, they perceive miracles as challenges, as puzzles to be broken down and codified until the
rules of logic apply and the mystery is solved. I believe that is
a noble, if futile, effort at escaping the human darkness. But it
is never done without a price to one's lyrical spirit. The humbling vastness of each breath of air in the midst of an ordinary
day is transformed into something to be tested, not tasted.

And that is what I believe that well-intentioned rabbi did
when he attempted to explain the miracle in the synagogue. He
took from his congregation the spirit of the experience. If the
role of the scientist is to try to demystify the universe—and I
believe it is—then the role of the spiritual leader is to embrace
the mystery. Neither will ever replace the other.

While logic is a cool light that helps us gain our bearings in
the cold darkness of the cave, myths and miracles warm us
from within. They keep us humble and hopeful. They enable us
to know how little we know, how little we control, how much
we need each other.

A few weeks after Lauren's service, I returned home from
work one night to the hand-over-mouth news that Nancy's
high school boyfriend Michael had cancer. In anguish I wanted
to call the rabbi and yell at him for taking away a precious miracle. It seemed we needed all the miracles we could get just
then. As Nancy and Michael found out at such an early age, we
know so very little about what awaits us around each corner:
what bumps right into us, what falls from the sky, what rum-
bles terrifyingly beneath our feet.

Seven years later, Michael is cancer-free—a miracle of science—
and the two high school sweethearts are still together and in
love—a miracle of faith. I am truly humbled.

In the day-to-day world of children and dogs and work and
rain and reason, where relativity and ambivalence guide and
temper our actions, myths and miracles give us moral certi-
tude. They are the rules of life, written miraculously in stone.
They are the visions of the prophets and saints, uttered without
proof, without fear that they would be shackled as lunatics.

Ultimately, a miracle urges glory and exacts shame upon all of us. It tells us we are beatific. It warns us of our insignificance. It lightens the way. Indeed, it seems to me that the very survival of our planet is dependent upon our ability to seek what is truly glorious while acknowledging the shame of overreaching our human bounds.

So, as one who in writing this is reminded of his own shame, I say shame on you, Rabbi. And, yes, Lauren, the Red Sea did part.

Idealism:
Reflections on Natural Discrepancies

> Our bodies can be mobilized by law and police and men with guns, if necessary—but where shall we find that which will make us believe in what we must do, so that we can fight through to victory?
> —Pearl S. Buck,
> *What America Means to Me*

Pasiano shared my wife's canopy bed in the Garden District of New Orleans. An ideal baby with pink cheeks, reddish-blonde hair, and stubby feet with spread toes, she was named—for reasons beyond memory—after a street in El Paso.

Thirty years later she was retrieved from a Duz carton in our attic in upstate New York and bestowed on the one daughter who had, by a devoted attachment to the menagerie that crowded her own canopy bed, shown that she would love Pasiano as fiercely as my wife had in the fifties. The decades had matted Pasiano's blonde hair and dulled her pink complexion. The lacy dress was yellowed and frayed. At her shoulder and thigh joints the material had begun to crack and rip. Of course, Clover loved her.

Patti and I spoke often of restoring Pasiano to her original beauty and luster, but a decade passed, and Clover grew up. (The eighties seemed to slip by like a ninety-hour work week.) A few years ago, though, perhaps in response to the broken dreams of children from Mogadishu to Sarajevo to Rwanda to Bed-Stuy and Detroit, I found myself standing in the seedy Poughkeepsie train station, Pasiano tucked in my knapsack, en route to the New York Doll Hospital on Lexington Avenue in Manhattan. Like Pasiano, the landmark train station has seen better days.

Clicking alongside the frigid Hudson, I imagined the metaphor of the doll hospital played out in the exquisite detail of an ornate Victorian dollhouse: the sparkling waiting room, a woman in starched whites and a cap who would cradle Pasiano in her plump arms and lead me into the office, a nostalgia-inducing room complete with a doll-sized examination table. The physician would be in a white coat, flushed cheeks, and a Robert Young smile, about to chomp into a shiny Red Delicious apple. On the walls I'd find a framed copy of the Hippocratic oath, a tiny sphygmomanometer, an X-ray viewer, a framed Norman Rockwell poster, and photographs of smiling and pouting dolls. At the back of the room there would surely be a door leading to the "SURGERY: HOSPITAL STAFF ONLY."

Stepping out of the warm sunlight on Lexington Avenue, however, I climbed a dark stairwell to the second floor and stumbled into what looked like a small appliance repair shop, dusty and frayed at the edges, cartons piled up tenuously, papers about to drift off every surface, dolls and doll parts everywhere. Irving D. Chais, the third-generation administrator of this hospital of cherished dreams, was not in whites or even surgical greens. He wore a plaid flannel shirt and faded dungarees; his hair was gray and ruffled.

The front room was a Mary Shelley daydream: upside-down doll heads lined the two shelves on the right; beneath them was a large carton full of arms and legs. In the back room where an assistant sat painting a head cupped in his bandaged hand, doll torsos hung from the ceiling like slabs of beef in a walk-in freezer. I recall a box full of eyeballs, but am not sure I haven't made that up.

In the fifties display cases—some open, some locked, all dingy—were a wide array of crowded woeful inmates. A 1925 Steiff bear was most prominent, though my gaze was drawn to a wooden boy staring straight up at the ceiling.

I handed Pasiano to Dr. Chais. In his able hands, she seemed more a curling iron than a little person. He nodded, set her on the cluttered counter, offered an estimate, not a prognosis, and then turned to me as if I were the real patient: What do I do, where do I live?

When he probed far enough to discover that I have seven children, he sighed, confiding that he had two daughters, but always dreamed of more. As he stood there in the middle of his own maudlin chaos imagining aloud the priceless, idealized experience of sitting down to dinner each night with all those kids, I knew that he would be as disappointed walking into my woefully disordered dining room as I was walking into his infirmary. As a gesture, I mentioned the skirmishes beneath the table that can make dinner seem like a battle zone. He shrugged and smiled as if he had a wonderful secret, and then turned to a lady with the beak of a cardinal, a thin Madame Alexander in her little girl's hand grown old with wrinkles.

I left Pasiano at the hospital and walked south toward Grand Central Station. I remember giving the last of my change to the first homeless soul who held out a palm, and turning away from the voices and fingers of the rest who followed, a demoralizing exercise in controlled compassion. One person, it seems, simply can't help everyone in need.

And hours later I stood in the gracious if somewhat seedy old Poughkeepsie train station, neck craned backwards, staring straight up like a doll, still wondering about the meaning of the doctor's enigmatic shrug and smile.

It was then that I noticed—as if for the first time—the landmark station's heavenly vaulted wooden ceiling. No doubt it reflected the architect's high hopes for something even grander than civilized rail travel along the pristine banks of the Hudson shortly after the turn of the century. If so, I decided with a scowl and a stiff neck, it was a failure. I glanced down and all around: from the sooty windows to the sticky floor to the homeless men on the gritty wooden benches, the depot exists as a stunning reminder that very little in this life turns out how we want or imagine.

I drove home in afternoon darkness to our rather lived-in house deep in the woods. From the rumbling van, which needed a muffler and a tune-up, I could see Nancy dancing in the living room, Patti at the sink, the lights blazing in all the second-floor bedrooms. The dog was happily howling at me from the front porch.

Of course, there were all the ordinary and extraordinary problems of real family life to greet me the moment I walked through the front door: the leaky toilet, Elizabeth's "lazy" eye, bills I couldn't pay, Clover's Lyme Disease. But from outside the white house with green shutters, I had to admit that it all looked like a dream of Irving Chais's making.

I wondered aloud if the good doctor had been telling me that the truth was inconsequential, that all that really mattered was the beautiful dream. Perhaps it matters only that we pursue the ideal in all that we do, something that ennobles each of us in our hard-fought and hardly-won lives.

"The stuff of dreams is not made for the future," I concluded, "but for the eternal present . . ." I had my finger in the air in mid-expostulation when I realized that if anyone in the family saw me they'd think I'd lost my marbles and try to have me locked up.

And perhaps I had, because in glancing to the side, I'm sure I saw Irving Chais, inserted like Forrest Gump outside the passenger window. He smiled and shrugged.

Inconsistency:
A Valuable Family Tool

> Speak what you think today in words as hard as cannonballs, and tomorrow speak what tomorrow thinks in hard words again, though it contradicts everything you said today.
> —Ralph Waldo Emerson,
> *Self-Reliance*

Over a recent Christmas vacation, the older kids—Cael, Nancy, and Addie—who had been slouching around the living room late one night, apparently ran out of college party stories and were then discussing how Patti and I had grown soft since they were kids wriggling under our iron-fisted rule.

Late the next morning the three of them were sitting across the kitchen counter like a tribunal of judges deciding on the merits of their parents' recent stewardship of the bottom half of the Lewis children. "You spoil them," Cael accused, pointing in the direction of the living room where Bay and Elizabeth—and nineteen-year-old Clover—were watching cartoons. Nancy looked heavenward: "Just look at how they take advantage of you. You never let any of us do that; you never let us watch TV during the day." Addie supplied the final nails in the parental coffin: "And it was never cartoons, just channel thirteen!"

Despite the fact that all three are old enough to vote, drink legally, and defend their country against enemy attack, they actually sounded jealous of Bay and Elizabeth, who were at that moment watching Scooby-Doo.

Of course they were wrong. In fact, as a direct result of the life lessons we gleaned in the expensive seminars expertly facilitated by their older brothers and sisters during the seventies and the eighties, Bay and Elizabeth suffer more wizened parental scrutiny than any of the other five who preceded them. Yet, demonstrating that iron will that I was accused of having, let me shamelessly contradict myself: in one rather narrow sense of family dynamics, they were probably right. I'm not as righteously protective of my kids' quality time as I used to be. Nor is Patti. We no longer see the great moral and intellectual dangers in sugar. We don't worry so much about whether they'll turn into ax murderers if they play with cap guns. We were wrong about the relationship between television and brain mush. We were clueless about the extraordinary benefits of boredom. We failed to understand that quality time begins only when the last child is asleep in bed.

I glared across the kitchen counter littered with toast crumbs, loosened my imaginary tie à la Rodney Dangerfield, wiped the real sweat from my brow, and in my most politically correct voice assured Cael and his doubly doubting sisters that, while we might allow the young ones certain liberties, "Mom and I are probably much stricter about things that really matter, like chores, homework, and table manners."

The darting eyes and smug little smirks on the faces of my three oldest progeny didn't need a translation. In case I missed it, however, Addie attempted an obvious explanation. "Good rationalization, Dad. You're just getting old."

Which left me speechless. In my own defense, I should say

that I'm not so far gone that I don't understand that any attempt to explain myself to my kids would leave me looking just a little bit older and stodgier and more stupid than they figured I already am. Better to look bad than feel worse, I concluded. So I wiped down the counter, scowling silently to myself.

A few minutes later, though, seventeen-year-old Danny woke up from his weekend/holiday/snow day unscheduled fourteen-hour snooze ("I need to make up for all the sleep I lose during school") and blindly stumbled into the kitchen. He stood in the doorway affecting a forty-five-degree lean, probably unsure of whether he was walking into a mall clad only in his underwear or about to be diving into a shark tank. " 'S' up?" he finally muttered to the sneering siblings. And once again the tribunal shared that same smug nod. Addie poked a finger through the air at her groggy brother. "Point in question." Nancy put an exclamation point on the accusing finger with pressed lips and a subtle shake of the head. And Cael made the final articulation: "You let them all get away with murder."

Which is exactly what Danny himself had said recently about Elizabeth. The resultant image of forty-seven-pound, eight-year-old Bishy as a murderer unfortunately left me bereft of my resolve to keep my mouth shut. "You know, we've treated each of you guys as individuals. You're all very different. Profoundly different—"

"Whoa, big fella," Addie pulled back the reins with a broad $3,000 Dr. Van Vliet orthodontic smile. "It sounds like we're being treated to a major contradiction here."

Had I known about Vauvenargues at the time, I might have quoted his *Reflections and Maxims* to my older smartass children: "If anyone accuses me of contradicting myself, I reply: Because I have been wrong once, or oftener, I do not aspire to be always wrong." Fortunately for me, I didn't know Vauvenargues from Vincent "The Chin" Gigante at the time, so I kept my mouth shut.

In any case, the principle of consistency is probably the

biggest myth the parenting smart set promotes about family values, childrearing, and so forth. *You must be consistent with regard to expectations, punishment, and rewards,* they intone with all the authority of a listing ark on the peak of Mount Ararat.

Of course, that's bull. Maybe a bull and a cow. Some kids need a strong arm to rein them in; some need to be set free; others need to be set free and then reined in as soon as they hop the closest fence. As Addie has been known to say, "Whatever."

While it is very important to be steady and consistent in your relationship with one child, consistency across the family board is not only unobtainable for ordinarily stressed parents, but a form of abuse to children who can't or do not need to conform to the standards of another sibling who needs them. Anyone who has more than one kid or had a sister or brother when growing up—or wasn't brought up by wolves—and perhaps even then—knows that everyone in every family is different. Profoundly different. That Danny can sleep for so many hours at a stretch is not evidence of his lack of moral fiber; he actually needs that much sleep. I celebrate him (as long as he gets his work done). In contrast, Bay apparently only needs six or seven hours to get fully charged, a scary thought. That's why when Danny was young and reading by flashlight under his covers long after his bedtime, I would storm in like an IRS agent and threaten him with long-term incarceration if he didn't get to sleep right away; and that's also why when Bay does the same thing, I smile and check my watch, just to make sure he's got enough time left to get the sleep he needs.

With Bay, we've got to make sure that he does ALL his homework, not just the homework he remembers. With Elizabeth, we must watch to make sure that she doesn't do more than she's been assigned.

The only consistent element in my out-of-order household is that no one turns out lights and everyone puts empty orange juice containers back in the refrigerator rather than crush them and throw them in the garbage.

It seems to me that what's terribly important to maintaining a healthy family existence is the ability to impart to your kids that changing your mind—for some reasonably good reasons—is a good thing. As Vauvenargues might have suggested, if you never change your mind, you risk making the same mistakes over and over again for the rest of your life. I pity those who would save me from myself—or worse, save themselves from me.

Justice:
Why Clover Is Still Mad at Me

> In the little world in which children have their exis-
> tence, whosoever brings them up, there is nothing
> so finely perceived and so finely felt, as injustice.
> —Charles Dickens,
> *Great Expectations*

The summer before Clover went to college, I asked her if she could recall the moment when she was most angry at me. It was an odd question, I admit, but you could see by the way she lowered her eyebrows and pressed her bottom lip against her teeth that she had zeroed in on an incident— *the* incident—without a second thought.

I was curious about her private anger, partly because I was teaching a class in autobiography and hearing a lot of memories about injustice in the silent world of childhood; I was also reading a book called *Healing Fiction*, in which the writer James Hillman suggests that much of our memory is fictionalized; and lastly, twenty-five-year-old Cael had recently accused me of ruining his NFL career as a kicker by not forcing him to practice a hundred field goals a day from the time he was eight years old.

Deep down I was certain that I knew intimately the angry recollections that Clover carried most deeply within her—a marinated guilt-ridden litany of fatherly insensitivities that had escaped my lips, punishments I had imposed, the times I was away, late, obnoxious, blind, deaf, dumb, clueless to her silent needs. And I wanted to apologize for the "big one"—whatever it was—before she left for college, before it festered and exploded like Langston Hughes's "A Dream Deferred."

But, as it turned out, Clover did not hold a grudge about any of my self-perceived paternal failures. What riled her the most—and apparently still makes her blood boil—was the February of 1984 that we were down in the Yucatán at the awe-inspiring Mayan pyramid at Chichén Itzá. Cael, Nancy, and Addie saw the massive and imposing pyramid and raced off to clambor up the steep narrowing steps to the top. Of course seven-year-old Clover wanted to follow them, but Patti and I were afraid that she was too young (and, I'm afraid, far too clumsy at the time) to make the climb without becoming a human sacrifice, so we said no.

That was it. She didn't say much in protest. If I remember correctly, and I hardly do, she didn't even cry. Maybe a little of the countless little blubberings that go on dozens of times in a seven-year-old's day.

And I was, no doubt, as smugly satisfied with myself as any two-bit politician would be who had just wooed a crowd with platitudes about making the "hard choices." After all, I was nothing if not her protector. I felt proud that I hadn't exposed her to danger. "Tough gazorts" (the Lewis family articulation of Tough Love), I probably said to her whining protestations.

But I was wrong.

And so our little Clover swallowed her public humiliation and the private rage of injustice on that intensely hot afternoon in the Yucatán, and then lived with a faint taste of bile in her mouth, an acrid reminder of life's unfairness for more than a decade before I asked out of nowhere about the root of her secret anger. And she was still seething at the injustice of it all as if we were still standing at the base of that pyramid!

I bring up this old "insignificant" wound now as an example of how important justice is to children. Small and powerless in the leggy world of adults, little children are sensitive to the core about injustice of all kinds. They stand passively defiant— eyebrows lowered, bottom lips pressed to their teeth—when adults fail to do what is right. Unfortunately, that is most of the time. Most adults are not concerned with justice; we devote our lives to "matters of importance," as the Little Prince says, valueless things such as money, fame, big cars, tennis matches, self-image, politics.

I should have gotten off my ridiculous high horse there at Chichén Itzá, taken her little hand in mine, and struggled (against my own clumsiness and fear of heights!) up to the top of the pyramid with her brother and sisters. I know from this vantage point that she would have struggled against the tight grip of my hand as we climbed those steep and narrow steps, that she would have been embarrassed by my shadowy presence at her side, but I also know that she would have understood what I was doing there. While there's no changing the realities of being seven years old and the fourth child in a big unwieldy family, she would have learned that justice actually exists through the good graces of people who can make it happen.

In a universe that seems to be as patently unfair as this one, it is imperative to act as if justice is attainable by human will. Without that foundation, children grow up to be cynical compromisers with puffed-up notions of acting in accordance with a dog-eat-dog world—or soft smoothies who want to ease everybody's pain.

Joie de Vivre:
Exuberance Is Better than Taste

> Exuberance is better than taste.
> —Gustave Flaubert,
> *The Sentimental Education*

The world may be divided into those who, when indisposed for any reason, will let a telephone ring until it's dead silent and those who would rather trample small children, flowerbeds, and senior citizens than let the same phone hit the magical sixth and final ring.

In our family, Patti and Clover, one with Southern aristocratic roots and the other capable of writing *The Lazy Woman's Guide to Enlightenment* but without the enthusiasm to do so, will simply sit there on the sofa (bed, floor, porch rocker, hammock, toilet, etc.) and let the phone ring and ring and ring and ring (and ring) as if it is not ringing at all, if they don't feel like answering it. They don't believe in the philosophy of THE BIG CALL or YOUR SHIP IS COMING IN or even the

Jewish-Italian version, DISASTER IS ONE PHONE CALL AWAY.

The rest of us in the family are true believers. We are resolute stampeders, including my new daughter-in-law, Melissa, whom I saw leap over a coffee table in her living room to get the phone on the third ring. (I was very proud.) Stampeders believe that every single phone call carries within it the potential for great personal reward: money, love, grace, salvation, or the perhaps most important individual triumph of all, vindication.

I'm not going to go into a long psychobabblous analysis of the two personality types. I bring up the distinction only to suggest that the day Bay received his first phone call ever, he introduced me to a third, more pure form of relationship to the world of communications.

Bay was in nursery school when the inaugural phone call occured. That meant two things: one, that he was too short to reach the wall phone in the kitchen, and two, that aside from conversations with himself on the yellow and red Fisher-Price beauty with wheels, he had never received a phone call from anyone except his grandparents.

I had answered the phone (in three rings or less, of course) and heard a tiny, tinny voice on the other end asking if Bay Wewis was there. It was Wobert on the other end. Realizing that this was a landmark event in my youngest son's life, I strode into the living room with a smile disproportionate to the event and looked around at the five or six expectant faces, everyone waiting to be called to the stage of their most telephonic dreams.

"Bay," I said ceremoniously, "Robert is on the phone for you." Which is when a fully exuberant, ear-splitting "YAHOO!" resonated through the house, drowning out the nearly audible sounds of disappointment that were exhaled by everyone other than Patti and Clover.

The entire family snorted in unison as Bay careened into the kitchen, lunged at the receiver lying on the counter, and managed what amounted to no more than a seventeen-second conversation while hopping up and down on one foot. After dragging a chair across the wooden floor to hang up the phone, he jumped down to the wood floor, rattling pots and pans, and raced triumphantly back to the family with undue pride scrawled across his little face.

Addie started the congratulatory fete by asking who Robert was. No doubt she expected that Robert was a friend from school and that we would receive a long-winded, goofy explanation of their adventures together.

So when Bay shrugged and said, "I don't know," we were all stunned into a most unusual family silence, even Patti and Clover, who actually sat up at the non-news.

"You don't know?" Clover asked in disbelief.

He smiled like the young Buddha he might have been in another life. "Nope."

"Is there a Robert in your class?" Nancy wondered softly.

"I dunno." Shoulders up and down, the smile like a warning beacon out at sea.

Exasperated with his brother and his questioning sisters, Danny scowled, "Well, what did he say?"

"He wanted to know what I got for Christmas."

"And . . ." Cael coaxed, "you told him what?"

"Stuff."

"And what did he get?"

"I don't remember."

A few seconds later, when the glow from my little guy's face was captured in the frame of his uplifted palms, we each realized that he was like no one else in the family. Neither leaper nor sleeper, the little boy was simply gassed that he got a phone call. He didn't care if his ship was coming in or his kayak was going over the falls or his rowboat was floating in the current along the endless river of life. It did not matter to him that he didn't know who Robert might have been, or even what the magical voice on the other end had to say. Someone—anyone—wanted to speak to him.

And thus we were introduced to unadulterated exuberance, a sheer lust for life and all its experiences. We bowed (briefly) because we were in the presence of the King of Joie de Vivre.

Admittedly, his reign only lasted until midway through fourth grade, when the feared conquerer, Mrs. H., taught him that exuberance was punishable. But along the way, charged up by nearly everything the fates tossed in his path, including food, movies, videos, soccer games, birthday parties, walks in the woods, and Sunday drives, Bay became a gauche Day-Glo reminder that life is to be lived passionately and fully.

The politicians and bankers and teachers and religious leaders in our lives invariably advise us—in grave tones—that we should, in effect, save for rainy days, keep everything in perspective, do all our homework, eat our peas and carrots, roll with the punches, pursue (moderately) moderation in all things, plan for the future, build upon the past, maintain the Sabbath, and floss twice daily.

But children remind us all that exuberance is indeed better than taste. Or good sense. As everyone's Aunt Edna says, "My candle burns at both ends;/ It will not last the night;/ But, ah, my foes, and, oh, my friends—/ It gives a lovely light." It is bright enough to light up the long and arduous path to our destiny.

Kindness:
The Not-So-Random Acts

> Human kindness has never weakened the stamina
> or softened the fiber of a free people. A nation
> does not have to be cruel to be tough.
> —Franklin D. Roosevelt,
>   radio address, October 13, 1940

The night Patti and Clover returned home from their dream-of-a-lifetime safari to southern Africa, we sat quietly on our dimly lit front porch listening to the crickets and peepers and screech owls in the woods. It was there that my mate of twenty-eight years told me that she had been transformed by the journey. She really didn't have to tell me that she had been changed, though. I could hear it in her new voice, see it in the new way she looked at me and the children.

At first I assumed that Patti was talking about some pulse-pounding experience with a lion or a rhino that must have brought her to the edge of death. But as I listened to the tales of their adventures in the heart of darkness, I found out that she was brought to the edge of life.

As Patti bounded along the dirt roads and trilling streams of her days and nights in Botswana and Zimbabwe, she told me that the most profound—illuminating—moment of the entire trip actually came just a few moments after their single-engine plane landed on a dirt airstrip in the bush. Gazing all around her at the vast uncivilized hinterland, and breathing in the scent of pure existence (in the form of a sprig of sage she brought back), she suddenly understood just how small, vulnerable, and insignificant her life—any creature's life—really is, how akin we are to the baboons that she had first seen scattering away on the landing strip. And in that moment of transformation, she felt not only utterly alone but an elemental part of everything at the same time.

Yes, there were the more typical heart-thumping, hair-raising, Discovery Channel safari experiences to follow that quiet and resolute moment on the dirt airstrip: sitting in the open Land Rover, Clover, Patti, and the guide were charged by a bull elephant; they once came upon a pride of lions at dusk; they paddled right alongside massive and dangerous hippos in the Zambezi River; they watched zebras mating. Yet all of that was only the glittering surface of the real truth—how cold and unrelenting and beautifully right is the path of the universe. In the midst of the vast Chobe Game Preserve, she knew that the soulful quest of the earth is not kind nor unkind, only balance and harmony. And the freedom she felt in her breast, she said, was like nothing she had ever known before, and like everything.

As the lightning bugs continued to punctuate the vast spaces created by her reveries, I too was transformed. Through her mesmerizing voice, I came to a new understanding of our remorseless planet and the human kindness that enables us to survive—and perhaps come to peace with—the shock of existence.

Kindness is not, as I had once assumed, the lighthearted random act advocated on so many bumper stickers. It isn't the smiley faces we see on nursery school windows. And it generally doesn't just happen on the spur of the moment, like a beautiful bird taking to flight or a gazelle suddenly leaping out of the bush. In the human family, kindness is instead a willful deed, an act full of intention and compassion designed to comfort some good soul lost in the merciless jungle. It is an imperative.

As Patti spoke into the night, my mind wandered off to the campfires of some remarkably kind and decent folks I have known along the jungled paths of my own life: David Demers, who for years took time away from family and work (and the ever-enticing couch) to read to a blind professor; to my old friend Teri Malkin and those long and bloody shifts she logged as a volunteer EMT for the local Rescue Squad; to Cael's old Little League coach, George Grammas, who translated the joy of baseball for young boys in his "free" time; my student the late Mara Weissman and her long nights at the crisis intervention center in Woodstock; David Jaman and his long days at the local hospice; and, closer to home, Patti and the way she's taught her Brownies to feel more at home in the woods.

As far as I know, aside from Patti, none of those good people have ever met each other. Yet they seem to share a credo about making the earth a little less random. Truly kind people seem to move through the chaos of existence without a sense of importance or entitlement, but with a profound urgency to take the hand of someone who is lost or alone or impoverished in the wilderness of our wonderful and scary lives.

I want my kids to be kind even more than I want them to be successful, smart, wealthy, or famous. What value is anything if it doesn't help someone feel more comfortable in his or her own skin? But, given the loving metaphysics of a parent's relationship to his or her children, I have never found a powerful enough fairy tale to read to my children that will spur them on to be kind. There are no how-to books, no New Age games, no school projects, no bumper sticker slogans, no rules or threats that really foster one's natural urge to do a good turn. In truth, I don't think we can actively nurture kindness in children the way that we nurture their young bodies. We're kind to others, and so our children are kind to themselves. They are kind to themselves, and so they're kind to others. Kindness begets kindness.

Sitting on the front porch that starless night, I saw, as clearly as baboons on a remote airstrip see an approaching plane, the imperative nature of human kindness. We must be kind because we are so in need of kindness.

Keeping a Stiff Upper Lip:
Standing Tall While Falling Down

> The man who sticks it out against his fate / shows spirit, but the spirit of a fool.
>
> —Euripides,
> *Heracles*

Despite a rather common and admittedly juvenile wish to be seen by my family as unique, charming, debonair, handsome, handy, sexy, athletic, philanthropic, and wise (and definitely over six feet two inches tall), my wife and children have had a lifetime of opportunity to see me in all my ordinary five-foot-ten-inch lack of splendor: love handles, crooked teeth, missing hair, empty wallet . . .

I should stop here as a gesture of kindness to myself, but, alas, I also have remarkably little self-control. Although my children love me (a truly wonderful thing to be able to write)—and rely on me for my various and sundry dad-like virtues—they have not escaped the vision of their father as a sort of nineties Dagwood Bumstead, writhing on the floor with my pants down around my ankles (trying, of course, to put my pants on two legs at a time).

Nancy actually had soda snorting out of her nose after I slipped off the edge of a six-inch-high gasoline island in North Carolina, suddenly disappearing from sight—and tearing ligaments in my ankle. Elizabeth was a giggling witness when a wasp flew up into my nose and then backed out and stung me on the lip. And Addie still talks about the time in the Agway parking lot when I attempted a manly hoist of a one-hundred-pound sack of goat feed into the gold Chevy Stepside pickup. Unfortunately, the drawstring was under my boot—I was first yanking against the weight and the unexpected resistance and then standing there in bohonk as my boots and my pride were buried in farming by-products.

There are no secrets in my supposedly private life. The children have seen or heard all the stories of Dad's stumbles and falls and wrenches and breaks that have over the years become an indelible part of their portrait of a father on the stumbling edge of eternal loss of face. As they have learned, I have found that real life is nothing if not a big tumble.

And thus this chapter on "Keeping a Stiff Upper Lip." Although many people tend to think of stiff-upper-lipness as the kind of brave persistence one demonstrates in the face of firing squads, natural disasters, terminal illnesses, mortal pain, and bankruptcy, I'm more inclined to see it in terms of the ability to keep on keepin' on after the kind of stinging insults to one's perfect image that all human beings endure on a regular basis.

As a teacher who has fallen backwards off a chair in front of his class, an athlete who broke his ankle while jogging out to the coin toss, and a writer who could découpage Rhode Island with his rejection slips, I have enough history to lip-synch right along with Ol' Blue Eyes as he croons, "Pick myself up and get back in the race." That *is* life, and it may be one of the more important legacies I leave for my kids when I shrug off this mortal coil.

In fact, on a recent afternoon when I was about to take Bay and his friend Luke to soccer practice, I saw the seeds of that legacy. The boys were right behind me as I nonchalantly pushed open the screen door onto the front porch and, thinking myself a gazelle, proceeded to show them my youthful prowess by taking the wide steps down to the path two at a time. Unfortunately, I hit that first riser at the edge and my ankle instantly gave way, my post-post-post-adolescent bulk crashing down the wooden steps to the hard bluestone slab below, where I proceeded to let out a hippo-like groan and roll my anguished way onto the dewy lawn.

As you might well imagine, I was in excruciating pain, writhing and cursing on the wet grass. Yet when I looked up to see my amused audience, no one was laughing. Bay had his chubby little hand on Luke's shoulder, gently moving his friend along to the car. Although Luke's head was swung back around in a mixture of curiosity and abject horror, I heard Bay reassure him in a most offhand manner: "Oh, don't worry about my dad, he does that all the time. He'll be up in a minute."

Luke apparently accepted Bay's explanation without question—and they waited patiently in the car for my pain and humiliation to subside. Of course, Bay was right. Rather than doing the seemingly mature thing and hopping my way back up the steps and into the house to lay my grass-stained leg on a pillow and ice the swollen and discolored ankle, I eventually uncoiled myself from the lawn and stood up on the one uninjured foot, brushed off the grass and dirt from my legs, and then hobbled and limped over to the Jeep.

Lurching into the driver's seat, I pushed a Van Morrison tape into the deck and cranked it up so loud the boys couldn't hear my pathetic groans. And twelve minutes later, they were leaping out of the car and racing over to the field, leaving me alone to mull my pain.

I was certainly a fool for showing off in the first place. And yes, some would say that I was a bigger fool for not taking better care of myself after the foolish deed was done. But I just kept on truckin', which is what most ordinary folks seem to do when confronted by their ordinary ever-humbling fate. Even as the pain in my ankle was short-circuiting everything I wished to be true, I understood that if I just stopped the foolishness, I'd be taking myself too seriously and Bay would never get to where he was going.

In retrospect, the meaning is as clear as the ice I applied to my ankle several hours later: a father leads his son into the next round of life's imperfect experiences and, simply by doing just that, shows him the spirit necessary to walk—or limp, or hop— through his own humbling circumstances.

Euripides may think it foolish, but it is spirit nevertheless.

Love
(and the Soccer Mom)

> Some are kissing mothers and some are scolding
> mothers, but it is love just the same, and most
> mothers kiss and scold together.
> —Pearl S. Buck,
> *To My Daughters, with Love*

If Hollywood and Washington, D.C. are related—
and it is altogether quite reasonable to think that
each one is the other's evil twin—then there is no
greater evidence of their kinship than in the joint
telecable promotion of our eternal vision of American Motherhood: Florence Henderson. For those
who have a difficult time distinguishing prime
time from nighttime, Florence Henderson *is* Mrs.
Brady.

Gosh, back in those good old days Mom was so
blonde and cute and perky and white and unmen-
tionably Christian and, of course, sexlessly
devoted to her hubby and blended family that she
just had to become the prime-time image of motherhood for all Americans. Week after week we just

loved the way Marcia and Cindy's mom was always a little bit harried, despite the eternally domestic presence of the amazing Alice, the unperturbable Mike beside her in bed (yikes!), and the inescapeable fact that, like her neighbor Ozzie Nelson, she had no discernible household duties and no outside job. However, Mrs. Brady always had a ready-to-wear smile, a good word, a light hand on a shoulder—and, of course, Alice right there in the kitchen to serve up warm brownies and cold milk when someone in the family was uncharacteristically blue. Mrs. Brady was there for everyone, even when it meant that she couldn't be there for herself. A Stepford Mother.

Fortunately or not, I have never met a mother quite like Florence Henderson. Unless I missed something over the past fifty years, she simply does not exist outside the plastic walls of my television console, which may be why so many mothers are confused—and guilt-ridden—about how mothers are supposed to mother their children and the various ways that love is expressed.

In fact, because like most dads I love the *je ne sais quoi* essence of my own family (and their peculiar ways) much much more than I might like the gorgeous bouquet of anyone else's family, I've come to believe that when Hollywood made the choice of Florence Henderson as Mother of the Century, they simply chose the wrong Henderson from the long list of prospective mothers of the year. If they had just looked a few names further down on the list of candidates, they certainly would have chosen Patricia Charlee Henderson (the girl I married).

However, I'm not so blinded by my own brand of love that I can't see that practically everyone else thinks that his or her own wife or mother is the best in the world. And in a sense, everyone is right, because no one can love you more than your mother, kisser or scolder—or both.

The soccer mom, who got a lot of media exposure in the 1996 presidential campaign, is a good example of Pearl Buck's point about the dimension of love. Just check out the line of folding beach chairs on the sidelines of any soccer field in America—or glance up toward the steely bleachers—and you'll see love expressed in the most extraordinary and indefinable ways. There is no singular soccer mom.

For the last twenty falls in New Paltz, you could predictably find Patti and two of her good friends, Stacy Schenker and Donna Ciliberto, rooting for their kids at some soccer game in town. Each one a soccer mom. Each one as different as one child on the field is from the next.

Patti is, to quote Ms. Buck, a kisser and a scolder, hard to pin down. As someone who goes to high school games to sit in the bleachers and talk to Stacy and Donna, she usually couldn't care less what goes on on the field. You will never hear her spouting metaphors about life and sport. She hates baseball, doesn't understand football, has little patience for basketball, and thinks there is something repulsive about wrestling. She does like soccer, though—and will cheer and scowl for her kids right along with Donna—but is often so busy talking to Stacy that she's not always 100 percent sure whether her children are on the field. A real mother.

On her right is Donna. For twenty-two hours a day, Donna Ciliberto is perhaps the most serene mother in this town. Blonde like Mother Florence and astute as Mother Nature, Donna seems to move through life with the composure of a Norwegian Mother Teresa. She is always on time to pick up her kids. She is rarely seen in anything but pastels. Cool, calm, and collected, she micromanages everything in the Ciliberto family from Frank's afterschool lawn business to Tony's college scholarship to Kurt's laundry to Jimmy's swimming career. Plop her down on a cushion in the bleachers at one of Devon's town league soccer games, though, and she is instantly transformed into a real *Mutha*. The normally soft, calming voice takes on so much gravel and fire and passion that you actually have to turn your head to make sure it's Donna, not Frank, rooting on his wrestlers or swooping down on the ref who happens to blow a call against her daughter. A real mother.

On Patti's left is Stacy, Jewish mother extraordinaire, who apparently lost her daily composure seven generations ago when the Hebrews officially walked out of the desert and discovered the South Shore of Long Island. Dressed flamboyantly in the finest in flowing Gypsy wear and adorned with more bangles and baubles than a Mardi Gras reveler, you would think that Stacy should be providing contralto counterpoint to Donna's basso barbs, yelling (and of course kvelling) her support for the golden child Keith (or Jonah or Sean or Bonnie). Yet this normally effusive mother, who no doubt does more hugging and crying and yelling and exuding and fahklempting in a single day than the entire nation of Norway does in a year—and who was, of course, never on time to pick up her kids—is nearly silent, turned forty-five degrees to the side, unable to follow the action on the field. Genetically woven into the shiny threads of her son's garish goalie jersey, Stacy simply cannot bear to watch a game where every play near the goal that Keith zealously guards is fraught with the potential for pain and suffering. Another real mother.

Patti, Donna, and Stacy seemingly have as much in common with one another as the fictional Mrs. Brady and the real Florence Henderson. Yet they love each of their children (15 in all) with abandon. On the field and off. Diving for a goal and falling flat on their faces. When the cameras are rolling and when there's no film on the spool.

And, most important, each of their children believes in the pulsing core of their hearts that there's not a mother in the world who loves her kids more. Not even Mrs. Brady.

Loyalty
(and Kinship)

> Though familiarity may not breed contempt, it takes the edge off of admiration.
>
> —William Hazlitt,
> *Characteristics*

Nancy, Addie, Clover, and Danny had made it clear in the van that they would rather eat raw liver than sit with us in the Nags Head Twin Cinema, despite the fact that I would be paying for their tickets and candy. And $51.75 later (which was so low only because of the cheap matinee tickets), the four ingrates sat two rows in front of Bay, Elizabeth, and me, munching popcorn, Twizzlers, Sourpatch Kids, and Gummi Bears, blithely pretending not to be related in any way to their blood relatives a mere six feet away.

Patti and Cael, who also were not showing much family spirit, had stayed back at the cottage in Rodanthe, feigning illness in order to get some peace and quiet while the remaining seven of us drove all the way up to Nags Head to see one of those instantly forgettable summer drivel movies from Hollywood on an utterly forgettable drizzly summer day.

The big kids didn't want to sit with us, they said, because Elizabeth would squirm and talk through the entire film, and because Bay would have to get up and go to the bathroom at least four times during the feature because he was drinking a Coke. I didn't argue with them, because what they said was true: Elizabeth would jabber incessantly and Bay would have to pee a lot.

But I was still miffed at their complete lack of loyalty and kinship. I knew that the talking and peeing problems were just handy excuses for the real issue: they simply didn't want to be associated in any way with the family name or looks when Bay or Elizabeth or I (yes, me!) would undoubtedly do something embarrassing enough to ruin their reputations in a North Carolina beach town 540 miles away from our home in upstate New York.

Deserted by our own flesh and blood, my goals for the movie were no longer to control Elizabeth's jabbering and Bay's attraction to urinals, but to gain some measure of revenge by tossing an occasional popcorn kernel at the heads of my older children. It was a safe bet that they'd never turn around to see who was attacking them.

As we settled into our seats and waited for the feature to come onto the screen, Bay was sipping the large Coke that he was to be sharing with Elizabeth, and Elizabeth was miraculously jabbering despite a mouthful of the tub of popcorn she was supposed to be sharing with Bay. All was well. Until Bay reached over for a handful of popcorn, and the giant cup slipped from his chunky paw, hit the concrete floor, and splattered all over his sneakers, instantly creating an icy brown river rushing headlong down toward the screen.

I didn't freak out; with seven kids there's been a lot of spilled sodas in my life. Besides, I was rather proud of Bay for wimpering rather than bawling out loud and calling attention to us. And despite the fact that I would have to go replace the thirty-nine-cent drink for $2.09, I took some satisfaction in the fact that the soles of the big kids' flip-flops were probably now coated with sticky Coke syrup.

Unfortunately, that was not the end of our travails. For reasons beyond my experienced understanding, when Elizabeth needed to see exactly where the cup had landed, she tipped the entire tub of popcorn off her lap and onto the wet floor. And she was not quite as gracious as Bay, yelping her great unhappiness to the entire theater. Of course, the big kids never even turned their heads.

I took the great big Dad-breath in order to silence the sizzling wires in my brain and managed to calm the little girl down by promising to get a whole new $3.50 tub of twenty-nine-cent popcorn. "And a new Coke for Bay," she added with a sisterly wimper.

"Of course," I muttered with a fixed slash of a smile.

A mere $5.76 later, I was back in the theater, one hand grasping a large Coke and the other hugging a giant tub of popcorn. Only it was dark now and the movie had already begun. I sidled into the row and was just about to hand Elizabeth the popcorn when I slid unceremoniously on a pile of popcorn that lay on top of a wet, syrupy slab of concrete, and my back foot slipped out from underneath me. Attempting to avert a crash landing of stunning proportions, I lurched forward for something solid to break my fall, but since both hands were full, the Coke was crushed on the seat back in front of Elizabeth, and, my thumb suddenly jammed in between the seats, I collapsed in a heap on my little children's laps. Elizabeth screeched. Bay laughed. A nice picture.

When the black box was retrieved hours later, and I began to recollect for Patti the events leading up to breaking my thumb in the crash landing at the Nags Head Twin Cinema, three sounds could be distinctly heard: a grown man squealing "Oh no!!!"; a dull "Umph!" as he bent his thumb back to his wrist; and an entire chorus of southern yocks and New York giggles and West Virginia howls all around the scene of the accident. One person, I remember, started laughing so hard she had to get up and leave the theater.

As it turned out, my free stunt proved to be a lot more entertaining than the utterly lame and expensive movie. Except, of course, to the four members of the Lewis clan two rows ahead, who, as I predicted, never once turned their heads to see what the commotion was all about. They knew.

I got them back, though, and in doing so made an important point about the role of kinship in the family values system. Before the four of them could slip out of the theater and race to the van and slink down in their seats, I blocked the aisle, told Elizabeth to hold Clover's hand, ordered Danny to hold Bay's hand, and put my sore arm and broken thumb around Nancy and Addie, respectively. And as we walked—I hobbled—out of the theater together, we were scrutinized by everyone who had spent the entire movie waiting to see what the idiot who spilled all that Coke and popcorn looked like.

And that's when my older children understood the truth behind the ages-old elementary school saying: You can pick your friends, and you can pick your nose, but you can't pick your friend's nose—or your family.

Manners:
Why It's Wrong to Belch at the Table

> Under bad manners, as under graver faults, lies very commonly an overestimate of our special individuality, as distinguished from our generic humanity.
> —Oliver Wendell Holmes, Sr.,
> *The Professor at the Breakfast Table*

After Danny, the present missing link in our family, let loose with a thunderous belch at dinner recently, six events immediately followed like a domestic avalanche:

1. Eight-year-old Elizabeth gasped, as much in disgust as in delight, while
2. Eleven-year-old Bay giggled hysterically, hand over drooling mouth, and then tried to cough up one himself before
3. Patti, whose face had instantly drained of all color, pointed the avenging maternal finger at the slovenly, ill-mannered creature who was once in the distant past her good little boy, and threatened

immediate grounding and loss of the car with the razor-edged "Not at the table!" as

4. Danny, who as anyone with any perspective could tell was rather proud of himself for such a manly Dad-sized (or perhaps Cael-sized) belch, replied with a smirky, "Excuse me," and looked my way for some moronic adolescent support, and then

5. I, who under different circumstances might have been eager to impart support in the spirit of male bonding, wisely chose to swallow my own sympathetic urges. However, with four sets of eyes trained on me, I knew that I was expected to deliver something on the order of a Proclamation on the Proper Time and Place for Acts of Oral Indigestion. Glancing all around the table and determining exactly which of the four sides my bread was buttered on, I finally answered my son in those deep gravelly fatherly tones that probably go all the way back to Abraham instructing the full-of-questions Isaac to just lay down on the sacrificial pyre. "Listen to your mother," I said, whereupon

6. Danny turned palms up in the universal pose of disingenuousness and asked the question of all cultural questions: "This is so messed up. I mean, what is wrong with burping? It's natural, isn't it?"

Yes, Danny, I considered saying, *burping is absolutely natural, a function of biology as much as a gurgling stomach or peristalsis or a sneeze or an itch or a blink, none of which require abstention or apologies. And yes, boys will be belching boys, although your sister Addie can belch with the best of them, as could a former student of mine, Melissa, who, if memory serves me correctly, could make the I-beams shudder at Dover High School. And yes again, in some cultures belching at the end of a meal is considered a supreme compliment to the cook. So I say, let 'er rip, boy!*

But fortunately I kept my mouth shut, saying nothing more than, "You don't belch at the table. It's not polite," thus betraying my gender but remaining true to my wife and to the principle that manners and humility are the keys to a well-lived family life.

Viewed at a distance, most manners are silly little rote conventions that have nothing to do with the pursuit of truth or justice or even the enjoyment of a good cheeseburger and fries. They are arbitrary social regulations that seem to appear and disappear in the most unlikely places, according to geography, class, gender, locale, age, time of day, and the age and weariness of parents.

Supposedly intended to make human interaction more civil and less contentious, flying the flag of good manners often provides a well-rationalized excuse for enslaving those supposedly less fortunate—and less perfumed—than ourselves. One backward glance at the history of the civilized world will yield a disturbing vision of the most uncivilized, inhumane atrocities committed by the most well-mannered persons and groups, often in the name of preserving civilization or saving souls. And despite the fact that good breeding and manners should foster a kind of democracy of spirit, in practice they simply tend to make some people feel superior to their cousins the apes and better than their brothers and sisters who live in smaller houses and tenements right around the corner.

As such, holding a door open for a lady does not necessarily mean that you are a good or thoughtful person, nor does calling an older person sir or madam signal your worthiness. Nor does refraining from belching at the dinner table suggest that you are in any way cultured. Each one merely shows your compliance to a worthy if superficial standard.

With apologies to millions of parents and preschool teachers who each day demand that children say the "magic words" in order to learn manners, every regular kid in the universe knows that *please* and *thank you* have little to do with good manners per se. In reality, children learn early in life that if they don't want to get hassled and if they stand any chance of getting what they desperately want, they simply have to say please and thank you to get it. Wally Cleaver's friend Eddie Haskell is the archetype of the well-mannered manipulative scoundrel who lives within each of us.

So why hold a door if it's such a hypocritical act? Why say please and thank you if their use is so disingenuous?

Because, if nothing else, the magical acts and magic words remind us that we are not entitled to anything at all in this world. Anything. We simply must ask politely, or sneakily, and then we just may get what we want so badly.

And the same goes for belching at the table. There's nothing intrinsically wrong with letting loose with a big window rattler, if that's how you feel. But the rule against situational belching, no matter how arbitrary or unnatural, lets each of us know that we are not allowed to do whatever we want or is natural to do whenever we want to do it. Manners exist solely to help us in the eternal quest to not get too big for our britches, which is the surest path to despair.

So, just as Danny wanted to get out of the house that weekend—or any other gaseous girls and boys want whatever it is they want—it is apparently up to their parents to curb their own adolescent urges and let them know that the next time they might want to let loose with a really big one, they might consider swallowing it like it was an insult to their mothers. Because that's exactly what it is.

Belch out in the woods. Belch at second base. Belch with your buddies. Belch at belching contests. Belch at the bar. You just may not belch at the table.

And don't lean back in the chair.

And use your napkin.

And don't use your fingers.

And chew with your mouth closed.

And don't interrupt while someone else is talking.

And stop making that noise.

And you may not leave the table without first asking permission.

And, as if it needs mentioning, keep your hands out of your pants.

Behave yourself. You are not as big as you think you are.

Mercy:
There but for the Grace of God . . .

> Teach me to feel another's woe, / To hide the fault I see; / That mercy I to others show, / That mercy show to me.
>
> —Alexander Pope,
>   "The Universal Prayer"

I glanced up. The watchtower made me think of the tree house back home.

Minutes later I was being frisked with a metal detector and led by beefy guards through several cinderblock passages, each separated by sliding steel cage doors. We filed into the prisoners' meeting room and sat down. "The Shawangunk Correctional Facility is a maxi-maxi," shackled inmate #91-8514 barked at us, "constructed for the worst of the worst in New York State."

I was not a new recruit, just a chaperone on a high school field trip, but I felt the jagged edge of his incorrigible pride. In front of the room, the inmate members of the Youth Assistance Program (YAP) stood one by one and told their appalling histories to Coach Ciliberto's Health Issues class. At some point, each of the lifers invoked the institutionalized mantra about how easy it is to get into *the system* and how hard it is to get out.

To say that they were bad men does not do justice to their depravities. One was a former Mafia big shot. Another was a serial killer. Tommy Two-Time told us how he slit one man's throat from left ear to right, and then from right to left. Thus the Two-Time. And in case we didn't get it, he went on to explain that he once blew a hole through a man's heart with his sawed-off shotgun—and then finished the already done job with another through his head. Tommy Two-Time.

Yet I had to remind myself often during the long, troubling day not to feel sympathy for these criminals. No mercy. Even when they spoke of the grisly slope that led to the ratlike, merciless conditions in which they merely survived. Even when they implored the class to stay on the straight and narrow. But as a deeply entrenched father, I couldn't help seeing the little boy behind each of their murderous mugs. Someone's little boy catching fireflies on a summer night, shooting hoops on a fall afternoon, playing in a tree house long before it all came tumbling down. Was there no mercy for these boys?

The culmination of the day was the tour of a two-tiered cell block. This was not the spacious if spare Mayberry jail of my TV youth, and the men behind bars bore no resemblence to any of Sheriff Andy's local drunks. The dim six-by-nine cinderblock cells are reminiscent of the dank indoor cages at a city zoo. As we edged our way along the nightmarish catwalk, some of the "worst of the worst" stood voiceless and glaring through the thick steel bars; others yelled cold obscenities at us.

And a few weeks later I could still feel the steely glares and serrated voices like splinters deep in my soul. To get away for a few moments, I climbed the homemade ladder up the ten-by-ten-by-ten tree-house deck, constructed around two shagbark hickorys and a fir. I then walked into the framed-out eight-by-eight house-in-progress, figuring again the placement of the screen windows and the door, imagining once more the parentless secrets and giggling indiscretions my two youngest children will share with their friends up in the trees by the stream we call Snowsoup.

This is the fourth tree house I've made over twenty-eight years of parenting seven children. The first never actually got built; it was constructed for our then only child Cael in 1971 as I lay flat on my back, fingers laced behind my head, on the patchy grass around our first house in Milwaukee. As you might imagine, it was to be a rather elaborate multilevel, accessorized Robinson Crusoe affair.

In making the second tree house in 1976, intended for Cael, Nancy, and Addie, I actually used a hammer, nails, and rough-cut lumber from the local sawmill. It consisted of a primitive platform and a kind of half-roof (don't ask) suspended somewhat precariously around two large and sappy white pines in our upstate New York backyard.

Number three was architected by the more craftsmanlike eighties me for Clover and Danny when we moved back into the woods. A triangular duplex with the deck right on top of the house, it lasted almost a decade until seven feet of snow made it structurally unsafe. I tied heavy ropes to the beams and yanked the whole thing down behind the lime-green Jeep, mud slinging back on my fallen handiwork.

Now, at fifty-one and considering posterity for the first time in my life, I'm fashioning number four. It should be finished (screened windows, door, shingled roof) before Danny graduates from high school and leaves Patti and me with a regular-size American family for the first time since late 1974.

As I stood up there under the awning of treetops, Bay, eleven, and Elizabeth, nine, joined me. They leaned on the railing, handing me galvanized nails and jabbering nonstop about the sleepouts and parties they were going to have up there. I was barely listening, though, pounding 16-penny nail after 16-penny nail into the pressure-treated pine, unable to escape the memory of the men I met at Shawangunk, most of whom will live the rest of their miserable days in cells smaller than my children's tree house.

Because I have seven children, people sometimes ask how to save their kids from going down the wrong path in life. I wish I knew how to protect kids from themselves. After seven kids I have learned just enough to know that there is no simple answer. All the usual buzzwords that flow through institutions like Shawangunk Correctional Facility—dysfunctional families, the welfare cycle, absentee fathers, self-esteem, etc.—might help to make those of us outside the prison walls feel safe, but they do not fully explain why one boy grows up to be a father building a tree house for his children and another grows up to be a killer.

From this vantage point, I'm pretty sure that the real question is not how innocent babies grow into criminals—it's not difficult to see the path from the trees. The crux of the matter is how anyone constructs a home that is insulated with enough love and mercy to withstand the kind of severe weather in the heart that drives boys and girls to the ground trembling with cold fear and icy vengeance, the kind that drives good children inside stark maximum-security cells from which they'll never escape.

When I turned away from all the pounding, Bay was telling Elizabeth about how he was going to jump off the deck this winter into the massive snowdrifts we sometimes have up here. And as a brisk wind shook the thick branches above us, I could almost hear Tommy Two-Time's voice cracking as he told the visitors about his bitter anguish at not being allowed out of the prison to go to his sister's funeral.

The two voices together were like an awful and lovely duet: two little boys, one weeping for his sister, the other telling her about his dreams. Have mercy.

Nonviolence:
Sorry, Kids, Spanking Is a One-Way Street

> When angry, count four; when very angry, swear.
> —Mark Twain,
> *Pudd'nhead Wilson*

In her earliest years, Addie was known around the house as the Bulldozer. Not because of the way she looked: a beautiful round-faced urchin in a smock dress and a baseball hat and a doll in one hand and a ratty ball in the other—and oh, those dimples. But because of the way that she seemed to bulldoze her way through the family world. While Cael and Nancy had learned early on to cope with the twin emotions of desire and frustration by sidestepping obstacles planted in their way, Addie invariably went right at—and sometimes through—whatever stood in her way.

In fact, on Adelyn's first report card, the teacher ended a wonderfully positive evaluation with the following caveat: "When frustrated, Addie tends to hit and tease. We need to help her with that."

And so we tried to teach Addie the several axioms of family life:

1. Frustration is unavoidable.
2. Although spanking under certain circumstances may be an appropriate parental prerogative, it is never okay for children to hit their parents, no matter how frustrated they are.
3. Never say never. It's very frustrating.

And as long as I'm tossing out axioms like they're hot dogs on the family grill, there is one other axiom of family life that we didn't share with the Bulldozer: the last kids to be picked up from Little League practice or play rehearsal or Brownies are the seedlings from large family trees. Just ask Danny's best friend Keith, the fourth Schenker to be left standing alone on the sidewalks of life waiting for Stacey to pick him up. Or check with any of the eight Bostwicks, who have never known the concept of timeliness. Or Joanne Archard's expansive brood up in Rangely, Maine, who no longer wait for their mother to show up; they just start walking.

Or you can just call any of my kids. Cael has a few stories for you. So does Clover.

Addie learned about the vicissitudes of late-arriving parents early in life. I was due to pick her up from kindergarten at 3:05 P.M. No problem. My classes were over at Dutchess Community College at 2:30, and it was exactly a thirty-five-minute drive to the Campus School. Perfect.

Unfortunately, at 3:04 P.M., when all the good and prompt parents of regular-sized families were waiting expectantly in their warm cars on Tricor Avenue, I was stuck in traffic on the Mid-Hudson Bridge, at least twenty minutes from my soon-to-be-waiting five-year-old.

I was late for a variety of reasons. I won't drive you down that road; there are always good reasons for parents being late, and none of them ever really add up. Suffice it to say that I arrived at the Campus School promptly at 3:30, terribly embarrassed, afraid the teacher was going to yell at me (a fear that doesn't seem to ebb with age!), but mostly very worried that little Addie would feel abandoned.

I jerked the car to a halt at the curb, raced up the concrete path to the tall glass doors, triple-stepped the entry stairs, and turned right down the long hall, sweating like a cold water pipe.

And there she was, my little bulldozer in her pink smock dress, way way way down at the other end. I waved and breathlessly called my apologies down to the teacher who was standing by Addie's side. The teacher hallooed back to me and said something else—a warning?—with what seemed to be a curious smile, but I didn't catch it because in a flash all I could see was Addie barreling up the long hall, a gorgeous smile of relief lighting up that dimpled face.

Ah, I thought as she raced my way, *she's not heartbroken; she's not crushed; she's not angry.* She's just glad to see her daddy. I decided then and there that I'd atone for my lateness by getting her an ice cream at JD's.

And with that, I kneeled down and the little dozer leaped into my waiting arms for a giant loving hug. Which was when I realized that she was sobbing under my chin. Which was just a second or two before she pushed herself back and began pounding her little chunky fists against my chest. Which was when I realized just how afraid she had been, how elated she had been to see me, how furious and frustrated she had felt to be forgotten, and how all of that was happening all at the same time—laughing, crying, hitting—all in equal measure.

Patti and I have never allowed our children to hit us for *any* reason. No matter how young they were or how extreme the situation, that is a firm taboo in our house. Although I've seen children hitting their mothers or fathers often enough at various preschools to understand that some parents—even thoughtful parents—don't place any real significance on it, I believe that children who are allowed to hit their parents are a step or two away from serious troubles in life. If they strike out hard enough to actually level Mom or Dad (a good shot in the gut or the crotch, for example), then the little pugilists gain a frightfully exaggerated sense of their own power; and if they fail to even make their parents wince after repeated round-houses to the hip or the upper arm, their powerlessness must feel soulfully profound.

But that afternoon, I allowed Addie to pound my aching chest while I gathered her up in my arms and held her close to my heart until she calmed down. It was—and remains—the only time I ever allowed one of my children to hit me.

I allowed it to happen because in this instance, no matter how silly or inconsequential it may seem to the adult mind, I knew that Addie was not old enough or wise enough to understand about chronically late parents. And the hurt she felt went all the way down to the dark core of her easily frustrated being—and cried out for the kind of balance that only hitting your daddy could satisfy. Sometimes you just have to balance the ledger, even if it's wrong.

The next time I was late to pick up the Bulldozer (and I assure you that she didn't have to wait long), I apologized profusely—and bribed her with an ice cream for my sin. But when she raised that little fist like a hammer, I snatched it in the air and led her most unsympathetically to the car—and right home. No ice cream. After the first time, she knew I was coming.

Nature and Nurture:
An Affinity with Your Animal Soul

> The roaring of the wind is my wife and the stars
> through the window pane are my children
> —John Keats,
>   letter to George and Georgiana Keats

Awhile back, the entire country experienced a teary-eyed communal "Awwwwwww" when a female gorilla saved the life of a toddler who had fallen into her habitat at a Chicago-area zoo. The remarkable event, captured by someone's home video camera, was instantly flashed all over the major newspapers, magazines, TV news, TV magazines: the mother gorilla with a baby on her back, picking up the unconscious little boy, cradling him in her long hairy arms, and carrying him over to the door where the zookeeper could get him.

For weeks we saw the endless scene bites: the mother gorilla, the boy lying on the cement floor, the crying human mother, the gates of the zoo, the zookeeper, the emergency entrance to the hospital, and of course the stereotypically dorky animal behavior experts at UI, UW, UM, IU, and MSU who were tracked down in their white coats, horn-rimmed glasses, and Hush Puppies and questioned about the unquestionable depth of compassion that the gorilla showed the little boy. Multicultural field reporters wanted to know how such human behavior was possible in an animal. Was it an aberration? Dumb luck? The hand of God? A prank? None of the above?

As Patti says, the only question worth asking is why everybody was so shocked. Anyone with a dog or a cat in the house knows that all animals are as tender, nasty, kind, rueful, compassionate, sneaky, and mortal as any person. They show us the substance of who we really are beneath the jewelry, hot cars, plastic surgeries, mortgages, and hair weaves. Which is why they are so valued in our homes. Which is why there should be a pet in every home in America.

The first time I recognized my own shared community with other animals was when Patti was pregnant with Cael. Our dog Tanya, a gorgeous collie-spaniel mix of some undistinguishable origins, was a great pal to both of us when we were young and unpregnant under the apple boughs. But when Patti began making any preparations for the baby's arrival, the dog grew decidedly morose. I'm not talking about losing the edge off her usual exuberant wag or having a little less bounce in her doggy step. I'm talking clinically depressed, as in curling up behind the old and dusty overstuffed chair (two dollars at the Madison St. Vincent de Paul) in the corner of the living room and refusing to come out whenever Patti started playing with the layette.

My chair, it turns out. The very chair where you could sometimes find me sulking late at night in the last trimester of the pregnancy, a little depressed and a little jealous and a little boyish because I was evidently losing my wife to Freddy the Four-Hundred-Pound Fetus. I'd sit there in that musty secondhand chair with a melting drink in my hand and every once in a while let out a lilting sigh. "Ah me . . ." it would have said if it had said anything. And then a few seconds later, like a distant echo from behind my evolutionary back, I'd hear a companion wimper, three short dog whines, which when translated would have meant something like, "You're not alone, pal."

I'd sigh. She'd wimper. I'd sigh. She'd wimper. I'd sigh. She'd wimper.

I always felt better the next morning, but unfortunately Tanya stayed morose. And while I actually recovered quickly (probably because I had better parents than Tanya), the dog grew so depressed after Cael was born that she camped behind the chair for days at a time, refusing to eat (or at least refusing to eat in our presence), and then, in a most annoyingly passive-aggressive way, refusing to acknowledge Patti's presence in the house. I was okay. Baby Cael was okay. Even the hated cats were okay. But Patti, the Jezebel, was not worth even a glance or a sniff or a wag.

And the cold dog shoulder continued on for nearly three months until one day she apparently decided that Patti had suffered enough. My guess is that Patti bought her a thick rawhide. Nevertheless, from our good dog Tanya we learned the humbling truth that animals are just as neurotic and manipulative as any human being.

Then there was Rachel, a gray tabby, the most ornery, miserable cat I've ever known. She had no use for people; in fact, she did not even like to be petted, much less carried or held. Through fifteen or sixteen years of a silently contentious relationship between the two of us, we had several brief if frank discussions—Rachel lounging haughtily in the windowsill as if it were a princess's chaise longue, me sneering like a prince reduced to serving his former subject—and right there and then we agreed that we simply did not like each other. Don't touch me and I won't rub up against you. Hissssss. There wasn't even a moment of remorse.

So it was a bit of a shock when, in her no-less-angry old age, the cat had a sudden change of heart about my lowly presence at her estate. Consumed by cancer, Rachel had recently laid down on a towel on the cold bathroom floor, thinly breathing, turning away from food, refusing to move. The first time I found her in my "office," I leaned on the doorjamb admittedly feeling more than a little peeved that the damn cat was going to finally get me by dying in the one room in the house where I could normally hide from reality.

Expecting a hiss as I made a step into the room (I was not going to be driven out by a cat!), she stunned me by starting to purr. Which caused me to step back at first, wondering if she had a plan to lure me closer and then, just as I reached down to pet her, scratch the hell out of me—a final act of contempt for her human enemy. Or maybe it was even more sinister than that; maybe she was intending to leave me a legacy of cat scratch fever after she passed on.

I snapped, "What are you up to?" But Rachel merely shifted her eyes and started to purr more loudly. And when I finally got up the courage to sit down on the floor next to her, she leaned her tired head against my leg and allowed me to stroke her bony fur.

For the next two days I visited Rachel often as she prepared to move beyond the confines of this life. Having never been friends, we didn't have much to say to each other. But I stroked the body that was betraying her. And she purred to my touch. That was it. I stroked. She purred. I stroked. She purred. And when she finally drifted away, I buried her beneath an enormous white pine and for weeks grieved every time I passed her empty windowsill.

In thinking back on those rare days, I have come to believe that Rachel allowed me to pet her out of kindness to me, not because she enjoyed being touched by a person. Sitting there together on the cold tile floor, she taught me that forgiveness has little to do with the person or animal who has done you wrong, but only with making peace with the universe. She showed me that to die with ordinary dignity, you have to make amends with life.

Open-Mindedness:
A Valuable Tool in a Hard-Headed World

> The beautiful souls are they that are universal, open, and ready for all things.
> —Michel de Montaigne,
> *Essays*

Years ago a rather sweet seventeen-year-old girl in one of my classes wrote an extended entry in her English journal about her evangelical religious faith and other matters of consequence in her young life. It was a thoughtful and poignant reflection on her relationship with God, boys, church, boys at church, the youth group, boys in the youth group, school, boys at school, the Christian college she'd be attending, and, of course, the boys she hoped to meet at the Christian college she'd be attending. The journal entry was full of all the marvelous and troubling contradictions of adolescence: one line written as a child and the next as an adult; a phrase full of clarity followed by a cry of confusion; eternal hope as a springboard to the depths of despair. And, as you might expect, vice versa.

At the point in the long entry where she began to proselytize a bit, she immediately retreated a step, apologizing for giving me—an adult, the teacher, her teacher—advice on spiritual matters. She worried that I would think her arrogant or conceited (which may be the most insulting thing you can say to teenagers about themselves), but clearly she worried more about the fate of my soul than about my ego. So, despite her fear, she plodded on into the darkness of the student teaching the teacher: *I know you're a good person, Mr. Lewis, and you've been so nice to me and you've taught me a lot, but I'm worried that you can never be saved unless . . .*

Unless?

Unless I would see the light and accept the Lord in the particular way that she had learned was the only way to salvation. Any other path and I would be lost for eternity. She had the road map right in front of her, and she knew that I was headed straight in the wrong direction.

Rather than feeling insulted or annoyed at her presumption about my faith—or lack of it—I was rather touched by her concern for the fate of my eternal soul. "What about all those Buddhists and Moslems and Native Americans—and all the rest of humanity—who worship God in a different way than you do?" I asked in the Socratic spirit one afternoon as I gave her a ride home from class.

She looked genuinely troubled as we drove up Franklin Avenue and out of the Currier and Ives village of Millbrook. "I know," she acknowledged, "it doesn't seem fair, but there's so much that we don't understand about life that we just have to follow what it says in the Bible. I have my faith."

I considered turning up the Socratic heat a notch by asking the usual tricky questions about forgiveness, but decided that shaking my young friend's faith like the limb of a sapling would not only be pointless but terribly unkind. So I told her about the time my father went to Catholic confession.

It was the summer of 1925 or 1926, and Samuel Levy, a street-

wise kid from the Lower East Side of New York, was busy trying to scrounge up some summer work. There were very few
jobs in the neighborhood, so when a friend suggested that they
apply for counselor positions at a Catholic Charities camp, he
jumped at the chance. "Just don't tell 'em you're Jewish," the
friend said.

It seemed like reasonable advice, and so he followed it to the
letter, making up a name and a religious history that didn't
have to be supported with anything akin to the facts.

And everything went fairly well during the first week of
camp in upstate New York. He liked his campers, his campers
liked him, the food was bearable, the grass was green, and the
mountainous sky at night was full of more stars than a city boy
imagined possible.

Sunday morning, however, he and his campers woke up to
reveille and the news (apparently to him only) that they would
go directly to the chapel after breakfast in the mess hall. And
that would have been fine, except that soon after entering the
country chapel and awkwardly following the little boys genu-
flecting and crossing themselves like baseball players at home
plate, young Samuel realized tremulously that there would be
no way that he would be able to avoid a visit to the confessional.

He sweated his way through the service and lip-synched the
sacred hymns, all the while trying desperately to figure out
either how to learn the most basic protocols of Catholicism or
get out of confession altogether. I imagine him considering
fainting—feigning delirium—maybe even sticking a finger
down his throat.

But when it was his turn, Sammy hadn't thought of any reasonable way to avoid the inevitable judgment. He was a blank
slate, a tabula rasa, a Jew in the Coliseum. He walked through
the folds in the curtain and sat down heavily, his young heart
pounding mercilessly in his bony chest, his forehead beaded
with the sweat of generations of supposed heretics before him.

The voice on the other side of the screen mumbled something
unintelligibly Latin. My father, who was years away from his

own fatherhood and who had been not too subtly eavesdropping on a counselor who had entered the booth before him, parroted the same words he had heard, "Forgive me, Father, for I have sinned." And then waited to be dismissed.

Five seconds.

Ten seconds.

Twenty seconds.

Thirty seconds later the voice on the other side of the screen sounded annoyed. "What is your confession, son?"

The air was as hot and thick and lumpy as the oatmeal he had been served just an hour before. He felt like he was being strangled. Out of the dark haze, he realized that there was nothing to utter but the truth: "I'm a Jew," he whispered and flinched, waiting either to be hit with a bolt of lightning or a fist from the other side of the confessional.

"What?" the stern voice quaked.

"I'm Jewish. I lied to get the job, sir, Father."

The priest's "Oh" was followed by another oppressive ache of silence, the whooshing of a robe, a clicking of the tongue, and waves of heat like the breath of Grendl's mother—and then a chuckle. A chuckle! And then a full belly laugh. And when the cosmic joke passed, he said, "Well, young man, that's a most unique confession. Why don't we just keep that a secret between the two of us."

I braked in front of a pretty house with a white fence, and turned to the passenger beside me. She wasn't laughing, but through a troubled countenance that looked close to tears, she wanted to know if my father was still alive. It was unclear whether she was relieved when I said he was, but her voice trembled as she opened the door and thanked me for the ride, and thanked me for listening to her, and told me she'd pray for me. And my father.

That night, as I lay in my bed with more questions than a man can hold inside his head, I felt comforted by the distant promise of a prayer from my kind young friend, and in turn prayed that she would find grace and, of course, lots of boys in the days to come. And in that dark airy moment before lapsing off this conscious coil, my father and I chuckled right out loud in the darkness when we imagined my young goodhearted friend falling head over heels in love with a Buddhist or a Muslim or a Jew as she comes to learn that the path to heaven is seen only through the open eyes of the forgiving.

Obligations:
Why Ricki Lake Is Not Welcome in My Home

> As states subsist in part by keeping their weaknesses from being known, so is it the quiet of families to have their chancery and their parliament within doors, and to compose and determine all emergent differences there.
>
> —John Donne,
> *Sermons*, No. 32

You'd practically have to be a zombie—or have been living in Theodore Kaczynski's rural neighborhood for the past twenty years—not to have noticed the cultural trend to air one's soiled laundry in public. From the traumatized children of parents who eat dairy products and pass gas to emotionally starved wives of working-class husbands who like to dress up like Ellen DeGeneres to humiliated boyfriends of girlfriends who sleep with janitors to despondent parents of sons who waddle, and daughters who refuse to change their socks daily, they all end up on Sally Jessy or Oprah or Ricki Lake, looking for some outlandish kind of

publicity and vindication for their particular brand of victim-
ization.

I suppose it is fun to be on television, although everyone on
those shows seems to do a lot of screaming and crying; and I
guess it may even be lucrative, although I don't remember ever
seeing any of those moaners spinning their stories off into soap
operas; and the de-visionary Andy Warhol did say that we
would all experience fifteen minutes of fame, although he didn't
necessarily specify what kind of fame.

But the price each of those informers pays for breaking
ancient family taboos against airing family secrets is to never
again feel safe in their own skins. Not even in their own homes
with their own families, the only people who know what they
really look like when they wake up each morning, before they
step into their worldly masks and costumes.

The largely unspoken rule in my family regarding truly
private matters is simply to circle the wagons around the particular family blemish and to use the obsequious-smile-as-two-
barrel-shotgun to ward off intruders.

Just as George Carlin identified the seven words one cannot
say on television (all of which have no doubt been said thousands of times by now), I would like to list the seven top family secrets never to be revealed outside the family circle.

1. *Bedwetting.* Most families have one or two (or . . .) kids
soaking their beds well into elementary school. Don't ask me
why, but it's viewed as a character weakness by outsiders, per-
ceived as an almost unbearable cross to bear by overlaundered
and overpsychologized parents, and experienced as deep
humiliation by the soaker himself or herself. Tell on your
brother or sister, and you open yourself up to lifelong retribu-
tion.

2. *Sex.* The most intimate and private, and thus most vulnerable, moments in two persons' waking lives sanctify their
union. Privately we are the vision of truth and beauty. Viewed
publicly, however, ordinary lovers resemble hairless baboons
making funny faces and gutteral noises. To pull up the shades

for public display—on a teenager or an adult—is to squander grace. Only your lover and your family know how beautiful you really are.

3. *Weight.* Since everybody in the family lies about their weight, it must mean something pretty important. Just pass on the lie. If you don't, it'll come back to haunt you, pound of flesh for pound of flesh. Guaranteed.

4. *The time Dad (or Mom or . . .) totally flipped out and . . .* It happens. It happens to everyone. To carry on the illusion of family stability, we somehow need to pretend that it only happens to the lunatics across the street. Keep it in the asylum you call home.

5. *Family feuds.* In any family, antagonisms abound. No one needs to know the particulars. Protected within the bosom of the family, every mother's son and every father's daughter ought not be made to feel uncomfortable with his or her own inexplicable and unsupportable jealousies. No one else will forgive you. As Bobby Frost said, "Home is the place where, when you have to go there, / They have to take you in." Enough said.

6. *Abject failure.* While we all love to revel in our siblings' failures, and many terribly misguided parents believe that revealing their children's failures will spur them on to success the next time around, and some devilish children like to use their parents' fumbling inadequacies as tools to gain sympathy or popularity with the local army of gossips, failure is as deeply personal as it is universal. After failure we need to crawl back into the dark cave of the family and lick our wounds. Ridicule results in the fear of being ridiculous. And the fear of looking ridiculous is tantamount to spiritual suicide.

7. *Who said what about whom.* This may be the most important of all the taboos. Within the four walls of one's house, people get to say the stupidest, most ridiculous, nastiest, shallowest, most ignorant and ill-conceived things about friends, relatives, and neighbors. The family may indeed take appropriate measures to in effect wash out the perpetrator's mouth with soap or even make a trip out behind the woodshed, but that should be the last place where the awful truth is told. To tell on your

siblings—or your kids—is an unpardonable breach of family trust.

That's it. Blab on about anyone you like who isn't related by roof beams. But if an outsider—especially one with a camera crew—ever comes knocking at the door asking for dirt on your family, I'd smile like a shotgun and tell her your family is none of her damn business.

Presence:
Why Bay Wants Me Home for Dinner

> There are one hundred and fifty-two distinctly different ways of holding a baby—and all are right.
> —Heywood Broun,
> *Seeing Things at Night*

My youngest son, Bay, asked at breakfast sometime ago if I had to work late that evening. When I glanced up from my coffee and told him I'd be home for dinner, he made a fist and (imitating sports yahoos all over the land) yanked it down with a whispery "Yesssssss!"

Ah, sweet fatherhood. Who else but a ten-year-old is so resolutely happy to have the old man around for an ordinary midweek meal? I went off to work feeling like the MVP of fathers.

All day I wondered off and on about what the little guy had planned for us—catch? a game? a drive to town for ice cream? Or maybe just some favorite TV show, his messy head on my shoulder, me grousing at him to get his sneakers off the couch? And twice that afternoon at the college I had to decline evening appointments because, as I told my colleagues with a shameless bragger's nod, my son and I were planning on doing "something special."

In contrast, Bay apparently proceeded through his fourth-grade rounds at the Lenape Elementary School without an idle thought to our plans. That night at dinner, the family gathered around the long pine table, he ate epic amounts of calories in a minimalist's minute, made indecipherable sounds (which might actually have been language) with his mouth full of potatoes and peas, and then disappeared down to the basement with his older brother Danny and younger sister Elizabeth as soon as they were excused from the table.

Which, in fact, turned out to be our only contact until I located him two hours later and told him it was time for bed. Whereupon we read a chapter of another scintillating Matt Christopher book, shared a moderately aggravating hug full of elbows and giggles, and he ostensibly went to sleep (which meant he got out the flashlight and checked out his baseball cards under the covers). Just like most nights around here.

That was it. I sank heavily into the living room couch wondering how I could have been an All-Star in the morning and a bench warmer ten hours later.

I concluded, a little mournfully, that there was apparently no hidden agenda in his morning question, which reflected nothing more than his innocent desire to know if I'd be around the house that night—much like a lamp or a bed or a mitt. He didn't necessarily want to have anything to do with me.

Of course. Why would a ten-year-old boy want to hang out with a fifty-year-old man, even if he is his father . . . unless, of course, he was trying to con him into buying something. I sank deeper into the soft cushions, grumbling just out of earshot of my wife, who is sometimes stunned that a man with seven kids doesn't know better than to indulge in such delusions.

And so it goes.

The daily realities of fatherhood are, on the surface, rather confusing and often quite humbling. I've spent a good many moments during the last twenty-seven years with my head tilted to the side like a painfully confused minor leaguer, wondering how it has happened that I'm a little balder and paunchier and perhaps even a little pastier—that is, a little more dad-like—than the sauve, debonair, windswept writer-slash-lover-slash-cool dad center fielder I once imagined myself to be at this dashing age.

And then a little yahoo like Bay (or any of the six others parked on the same familial bench who have also somehow forgotten my glory days) yanks me right out of the game in the late innings for not paying attention to the count.

The long, lonely walk to the showers that night was full of the once-implausible realities everyone finds at the bottom of their barrels. But when I slouched out of the steamy bathroom, Bay was standing there, waiting for me. He said he had had a bad dream. I put my arm around his thin shoulders, and we walked together back to his room.

Tucking him in, I asked my little boy about the dream, but he was too groggy—or maybe he just didn't want to talk about it. "I was being chased," was all he said. And then he pulled on my hand, urging me to the mattress. I asked again if he wanted to talk about the nightmare, but he just shook his head and curled up under the quilt that Patti had made for him. He fell back asleep still holding my hand.

He just wanted me around.

Of course. I'm his daddy. I'm a monument to eternal presence in his life, nothing more and nothing less. (Perhaps like one of the monuments in center field at Yankee Stadium, I wondered wistfully in the hall, and started to whistle, "Take me out to the ballgame . . .")

Like many other parents I've known, I sometimes think I have to earn my way into my children's hearts. I have to take them to fun and exotic places; bring expensive presents home when I've been away; have a constant stash of Jolly Ranchers in my pocket; take a dive after playing endless hours of Monopoly or Battleship with a smile; drive them anywhere, anytime, for any reason; and wave them off with a smile when they're old enough to drive themselves out of our lives.

But, as Bay reminded me, all children really want from their parents is to be around. Whether it's our oldest son, Cael, who's grown up and living in North Carolina, or Elizabeth, who's in third grade, the first thing any of my kids ask when they walk in the house and see me standing alone is, "Where's Mom?" And lest you think I'm chopped liver, if the only person they see is Patti, they ask immediately, "Where's Dad?"

Well, here I am. Apparently right where I'm supposed to be: on the sidelines like a Little League coach figuring out the lineup, offering unsolicited directions when they're running the bases, snarling when they get doubled up, smiling like I did something right when they slide safely into home plate for dinner (and passing the salt and cutting the meat). That's it.

And in return, it seems, I receive their undying, unwavering, uncompromising, unadulterated, unearned, unbounded, uncommon, undaunted, unasked-for love. To which I'd like to make a big fist and yank it down like a first-class yahoo and say, "Yessssssss!"

Purpose:
It Could Save Your Life

> Many persons have a wrong idea about what consti-
> tutes true happiness. It is not attained through self-
> gratification but through fidelity to a worthy purpose.
> —Helen Keller,
> *Helen Keller's Journal*

Sam Lewis, the former emir of wholesale school supplies on eastern Long Island, once proudly explained to his bleary-eyed eighteen-year-old son how the paper and pencils and flash cards that filled his small warehouse in New Hyde Park would someday help children learn to read and write. A good life, he suggested with a wave of a cigar, was bound as if by heavy-duty strapping tape (aisle 5) to the notion of purpose. A man had to have purpose. He then pointed the snuffed ember at a rusty boxcar that I was to spend the day unloading.

My father, born in 1908, was the third of seven children raised by immigrant parents. If the Lower East Side of Manhattan was his playschool,

and World War I pretty much comprised his elementary education, then the Great Depression formed his collegiate values. It
was then that he—and most other Americans—reckoned
mightily with the sometimes mutually exclusive concepts of
making a living and serving a social purpose.

I took my father's lesson about purposeful living to heart,
moving several tons of construction paper and then purposely
running as far as I could get away from New York. I went all
the way to Madison, Wisconsin, where I was going to learn to
be a writer.

Back home the following Thanksgiving, I argued that a good
poem or story could save a person's life. My father chewed on
his panatela, muttered that it would have to be a miracle, and
demanded that I put some business courses in my curriculum.
I told him that I flatly rejected all mundane labor practices—
and walked out of his house and drove off in his car to seek my
own purpose as a bard.

It probably did not help that my first literary efforts
appeared in magazines with names like *Modine Gunch* and *Road
Apple Review.* Or that my first poetry chapbook (New Erections
Press, 1969, of course), which was not reviewed, sold barely a
couple of dozen copies and paid me handsomely in contribu-
tor's copies. I opened my empty wallet and concluded that
writing was not only purposeless, it was profitless. And with
the old man's lesson still coursing through my veins like a
genetic infection—it turns out that even extreme Midwestern
cold cannot kill viruses—I soon grew to fear in my wandering
heart that there wasn't a book in the universe that could dig a
ditch or perform an appendectomy or save a life or supply a
child with the paper and pencils necessary to learn.

And thus I turned to teaching, a methadone clinic for writing
addicts. As an educator, I figured I could make a living, still
have time to write, and never question whether my existence
had purpose. Yet over the next twenty-five years, while I happily mentored several thousand students—and my own free-
lance writing actually became profitable—the old question of
self-indulgence continued to gnaw at me. I often wondered if

the precious time I employed pounding on a keyboard could have been more purposefully spent doing something of greater value to humankind. I read and reread Marianne Moore's damning pronouncement: ". . . there are things that are important beyond all this fiddle." I despaired that I'd ever write something as lovely—or as functional—as a tree.

Then, like a postmodern *deus ex machina*, my editor Julia Serebrinsky faxed me a front-page article she received from the Marion, Indiana, *Chronicle-Tribune* with the headline BOOK SAVES MAN FROM BULLET WOUND.

And my pulse quickened as I read about twenty-seven-year-old Shenandoah "Shane" Maxey, who was coming home from work one day when he heard a gunshot and suddenly felt a sharp pain in his arm. "It felt like someone punched me really hard in the arm."

Someone, perhaps his ex-wife, had shot at Mr. Maxey with a .22-caliber gun. But before the bullet had shattered bone or severed an artery, it struck and burrowed into a book Maxey was carrying in an insulated lunch bag that he had slung over his shoulder. And it wasn't just any book. It was MY book—*Zen and the Art of Fatherhood: Lessons From a Master Dad*!

"I was reading that book in hopes of becoming a better father," Maxey was quoted as saying. "Now I'm really glad I bought that book."

Me too. The news felt like a big shot in the arm from my proud eighty-nine-year-old father, to whom I immediately mailed a copy of the article so that he'd know that the miracle had finally occurred. (I also sent Mr. Maxey a new copy of the book to replace the one with the hole, the one that probably belongs in the lunch bag all the time.)

And now that it's actually been shown that writing constitutes a purposeful life, my good friend Myron Adams told me that he's considering making a line of flak jackets insulated with copies of *Zen*. He says we might be able to market it to families who live or work in bad neighborhoods.

Quid Pro Quo:
Giving Is Not Necessarily Better than Receiving

"All virtue is summed up in dealing justly."
—Aristotle,
Nicomachean Ethics

It's early October up here in the Shawangunk Mountains. Frost on the windshield each morning. Underdressed, goose-bumped, apple-cheeked kids jumping up and down at rural bus stops. Apples in lunch boxes, apples in crates along the side of the road, apples dangling from trees. Trees just beginning their spectacular dance. Children faking sickness in order to stay home from school.

Nancy was the first of our kids to try to fool us into letting her skip school for that vast melange of impossible-to-prove illnesses that can slip right through the cracks of a flu diagnosis: headache, sore throat, bellyache, achy joints, fatigue so extreme they can hardly walk from the bedroom to the bathroom. Take your pick. When challenged about the actual truth of her medical complaints,

Nancy often moved on to the asthmatic's ace-in-the-hole, ". . . and I think I'm starting to wheeze." In his heyday, Danny's last resort was the threat of puking on the bus. And now Bay wells up with profound grief whenever we don't believe him. It's as if he's been callously abandoned by parents who won't hear the agonizing pleas of their most innocent child.

As these things go in our family, sometimes the kids win and sometimes we win. And although Patti and I are rarely fooled by their ridiculous overacting, it does seem that every once in a while it's a good idea to just play along with their devious schemes. After all, kids, like adults, need a day off periodically to recharge their batteries. Plus, when children think they have finally swindled a day off from their dumb-as-mud parents, they're so loving and friendly and good-natured and helpful— because of course they're not sick—that they're actually fun to have around. It's a nice exchange.

I was thinking about this unspoken charade a few Fridays ago when Bay faked a sore throat and, after watching TV all day, accompanied me into town in the late afternoon to go to the post office. That's when we sighted the first Leafers of the year.

They were Manhattan Leafers, distinct from Jersey Leafers and Long Island Leafers. And they were easily identified walking toward the Range Rover parked halfway off the side of Mountain Rest Road. (Just for the record, LI Leafers typically commandeer Jeeps and park in ditches; Jersey Leafers just stop their IROCs right in the middle of the pavement.) The female Leafer wore the distinctive Patagonia jacket and fanny pack accessory just above the pubis. The rutting male was in a dark green Woolrich and sported the brightly colored toddler in a Gerry Pack. All three wore Timberland boots.

I growled up the standard Mid-Hudson Valley groan as I passed by. Admittedly, three downstaters gawking apprecia- tively at spindly overachieving maples flaunting their stuff this early in the fall is not a problem, but the first sighting always means that thousands of others will soon be flocking up to the mountains like tour buses full of rubes swarming around the World Trade Center on spring weekends.

Honestly, they create havoc among us townies. They jam Main Street with their various four-wheel-drive urban assault "NO RADIO" vehicles. They dig up wildflowers. They ride their mountain bikes four abreast on country roads. They buy up all the copies of the *New York Times* on Sundays. They practically molest the vegetables at the roadside stands. They destroy more trees at Pic-Ur-Own orchards than ice storms. They snicker at prices in local antique stores as if this is a Third World nation. They complain about the local Chinese takeout, the distressing absence of arugula, the regular-run movies up at the Plaza. They overenunciate when asking directions, as if we're not fluent in English. When they think we're not listening, they say, "It's pretty, but I'd go absolutely berserk if I lived up here. . . ."

Of course, it's very tempting to give them a big fat piece of your hillbilly mind—tell 'em what for—just as it's difficult to let your kids think they've fooled you again. But most of us shake our shaggy heads as the invasion begins and then race off to cash in on the bounty of the season. The local apple farmers immediately exchange their Calvins and Nike Swoosh T-shirts for overalls. And I've noticed more than a few of my well-heeled neighbors down on Springtown Road racing off to their attics and barns for their annual ad hoc yard sales.

We welcome the Leafers into our backyards year after inexorable year like distant relatives in for the holidays. We smile at one another the way children smile at cheek-pinching aunts. They patronize our clumsy attempts at haute cuisine. We relent and talk chainsaws and huntin' when they show up in creased overalls to buy rusty farm tools.

Up here we endure one another when the enduring's good, and smile when the last leaf has fallen. Down there, they puff grandly on their Cubans, count the take from all the genuine Rolexes we buy in Times Square each spring, and enjoy the quiet when everyone's up here gawking at the leaves. Up here we know that all that weekend capital helps pay the mortgage. Down there they know that the mountains and the colors keep them sane.

There is a wonderful symmetry about it all that suggests the ways in which we all get along by going along. Just like kids coming down with school flu. It's a unique psycho-eco-political-environmental arrangement that a lot of families—and nations—around the globe might want to look into. Quid pro quo.

Quietude:
How to Treat Houseguests

> To bear all naked truths, / And to visage
> circumstance, all calm, / That is the top of sover-
> eignty.
>
> —Keats,
> *Hyperion*

"How do you find New Orleans, Steven?"
Patti's grandmother says. She says it just like Patti:
New AW-yuns, with just a taste of an "L" in the
hyphen, not New Or-LEENS, like we say up north.
The sixteen-foot faded silk walls and enormous
shuttered windows dwarf the five of us seated at a
cherry table that seems as long as a bowling alley
back home at Mineola Lanes. I'm at one end.
Grandmother is all the way down the other side
near the pins. Patti's to my right. Her parents,
Nancy and Charles, are to the left. It is spring
break 1968, and I'm just about to learn the gracious
way to welcome any newcomer to the family circle
(especially if he doesn't understand the rules).

I have just arrived from New York to meet my

fiancée's decidedly wary family and still feel light-headed from the tropical heat in the Delta. "I actually haven't seen much yet . . ." I start, unsure of where to go to impress the matriarch. Like a cloud drifting across a pool, disapproval suddenly darkens the old woman's remarkably clear eyes. I glance over to beautiful long-haired Patti, who has a wry smirk on her lips. "Steven was just saying how beautiful the Garden District is, Grandmother."

Under the old woman's unyielding gaze, I nod, "Definitely. Definitely." Like a bobble-headed doll in the back of a Plymouth Horizon, I'm still nodding after the words have escaped my dry mouth.

She presses her thin wet lips into a smile and turns, white head tilted toward her granddaughter, who, knowing well the cue, places the napkin on her lap and moves the conversation toward flower arrangements and out of town guests for the wedding. The still air makes breathing a chore. My forehead is flushed, my uncombable hair is frizzing into a hippie beehive.

I am here to meet Patti's other grandmother. Not Damma, the one who likes the way I smell, but the wealthy cultivated one everyone in the family referred to as Grandmother or Tante. She lives in a gracious home in the Garden District, the front glass and iron doors as tall as my parents' rancher on Long Island. A tall man named Irving drives her around New Orleans in a massive black Cadillac with a heavy brass buffalo on the hood.

I recognize Irving as he interrupts the stilted conversation by walking into the dining room carrying a huge silver tray. He stops behind each shoulder and serves the grits, the veal, the dark gravy, and then finally the asparagus. I smile cautiously and almost utter thank you, but as I have never been served by a butler, I don't know what is correct. Irving doesn't seem to notice; he just moves to the left until everyone has been served, whereupon he quietly disappears into the kitchen.

Above the elegant dining room table is the kind of polite conversation and clinking of silverware on blue and white floral plates that I'd seen in Cary Grant movies. Underneath the table

I am sitting in a puddle of sweat, my right leg bouncing up and down like a piston.

Which is when my shoe slips a few inches and bumps right into something like a block fastened to the parquet floor. Carefully, I feel all around the protrusion with the toe of my shoe. It is round, not square. I very tentatively put my foot on top of it. I tap once. I tap twice.

And then, as if to remind me that I should be eating, not toeing a block on the floor, the kitchen door swings open behind me and Irving reenters with a tray full of serving platters. Once again he proceeds left around Grandmother, but no one is interested in seconds. He retreats back to the kitchen. Odd, I think, but as I don't know any better, I assume it's the way things are done down South.

Which is when Grandmother asks me what I am studying at the University of Wisconsin. Unable to eat and impress at the same time, I put my knife and fork down and articulate my well-considered plans to support her granddaughter on my earnings as a poet and occasional teaching "gigs" at colleges. She nods and smiles like I am the biggest fool who has ever sat down at her table.

At this point I am sweating like a guy in a forties gangster movie tied to a hard wooden chair positioned right under a metal lamp. As you might imagine, my leg has resumed bouncing at warp speed. And again I bump into the block or the knob or whatever it is on the floor again. I'd love to just lean over, lift the tablecloth, and check it out, but even I know that disappearing under the table simply isn't polite. Besides, Grandmother has just asked me a question I did not hear and is now looking my way, patiently awaiting a reply. The air is so still and heavy that I think I might suffocate.

Which is when Irving, the angel of mercy, appears once again to save my sweltering skin by walking back into the dining room. Because of my position at the head of the table, all I can see is Grandmother, who at first looks a little perturbed at the interruption, then opens her eyes wide as if she is studying something over my head. But the only thing the matriarch utters is, "Thank you, Irving. I don't think we are ready just yet." Her voice is gentle, the smile gracious.

I am totally clueless. When my scurrying eyes find Patti for an explanation, she glares at me and twitches her head as if she has swimmer's ear. I wonder if I am using the wrong fork or am chewing with my mouth open, but I don't think I've had a bite to eat yet. So I shrug. She presses her long graceful index finger to the table and taps it three times. So I take my fork off the plate and lay it down on the table, sweat pouring off my forehead, my shirt stuck to my back.

A half hour later—and two more pointless visitations from the butler and a sharp kick above the ankle from ever-playful Patti—the ordeal is over. I sneak a smile over to her like we're sharing a secret I haven't quite figured out.

"What a lovely breeze," Grandmother says, laying the napkin on the tablecloth. Everyone agrees, although I don't feel a thing except relief, convinced that there obviously isn't a breeze or a breath of fresh air for a thousand miles.

As Patti and I left the grand house that night and walked hand in hand along the uneven bluestone sidewalks in the beautiful Garden District, she explained between snickering cackles and bent-over howls that the reason Irving kept showing up when he wasn't wanted was because I kept hitting the damn butler bell with my foot. (So that's what it was!) And at that moment, I could finally feel the breeze that Grandmother mentioned so blithely. But it wasn't quite so pleasant as the old lady suggested, a cool shiver of humiliation snaking up and down the back of my soaking wet neck.

Not a word was ever spoken about my ignorant blunder. Not by my future in-laws or the gracious sovereign, who also understood that after a lesson is learned, there is no point in bringing it up again. I realized that night that if I had picked up the salad with my fingers (not me!) or swilled down the contents of the finger bowl (I did not!), my host might have done the gracious thing and followed right along to make sure I was comfortable. There is no point in humiliating anyone whose intentions are honorable. (And it's probably dangerous to humiliate anyone whose intentions are not.) In matters of household guests, it is better to be inviting than right, which is the essence of quietude at the core.

Patti and I have tried to bring that extraordinary restraint to the raising of our own seven blunderers and the social improprieties they and their friends bring to our good table. But we're still learning, and unlike Patti's grandmother, we sometimes neglect to notice the cool breeze and still end up getting a little hot under the collar.

Resilience:
Keeping the Course

> We may be masters of our every lot / By bearing it.
> —Virgil,
> *Aeneid*

Of course it's terribly important to learn to roll with those unexpected sucker punches in life (see "Keeping a Stiff Upper Lip"). And to be able to roll with laughter when life sends you stumbling to the canvas (see "Rib-Tickling") is a much undervalued tool. But it is also imperative to the righteous spirit to know that if something is truly meaningful, you are at heart resilient enough to put your good shoulder to the wheel and, as the Doors' decidedly unrighteous Jim Morrison once sang, "Break on through to the other side."

Whenever I've heard those old licks recently, I've thought of a young woman I have known since she was an infant, the older daughter of my lifelong friend Richard. Not only did Ruby Crescent survive a month-long coma at eighteen—after a hideous car accident on a rain-slicked parkway—

but throughout her recovery she resolutely insisted on living her life on her own terms—sometimes regardless of the wishes, warnings, and prohibitions of her well-meaning but anxious father. She got back into the car and put her shoulder to the wheel. She has moxie.

So does Elizabeth. Born with a profound form of congenital hip dysplasia that has dominoed to affect practically every aspect of her young existence, our cute, pigtailed, enthusiastic little girl breaks on through like a beefy fullback every single day of her life.

But I first met true resilience years ago when Patti was eight months pregnant with Cael. She was not much older than Ruby at the time. And on a deceptively sunny morning in June, when all that lay ahead of her was a dreamy summer day on Lake Kegonsa, her Uncle Bruce phoned from New Orleans to sputter out between deep sobs that her mother had just passed away.

Nancy Sharp Henderson was forty-nine years old, much too young to die.

Her daughter Patti was barely twenty-two, a college junior, married less than ten months. Some would say too young to be married and expecting a baby. Certainly too young to be pregnant and so suddenly orphaned. To this day I can only imagine the depths of grief and loneliness, the flush anxiety and cold betrayal that must have shuddered across her round belly when she heard her uncle's most final words.

We never plan for tragedy, just happiness, though neither is in the least bit predictable. Just six months before that transforming day in June, Patti and I spent Christmas in New Orleans, racing like teenagers around the Quarter, returning piles of pointless wedding presents, picnicking in Audubon Park, and dreaming of the perfect life we would make for our perfect child in her perfectly soft and round belly. I remember sitting in the kitchen with her mother, drinking thick CDM chicory coffee and talking—like the adult I one day hoped to be—about baby furniture and finances and plans for the future.

No more than a few days before her mother's death, Patti

was lugging her large self up Bascomb Hill at the University of Wisconsin to take final exams she cared little about. Her head was full of crib colors, layettes, Lamaze exercises, breastfeeding, baby names, the pain of labor, and all the concerns about heat and sleep that trouble all pregnant women in the summer. Not death. Not loneliness. Not grief.

Not how she would manage to navigate her way toward motherhood without a mother. Every woman pregnant for the first time needs a mother to guide her along paths she wouldn't necessarily take by herself. She needs a mother to comfort her in ways that she could not ask to be comforted by a friend, to offer advice that she wouldn't take from a sister. The humbling truth I learned during those unforgettable days is that she needs her mother in some ways more than she needs her young and painfully confused husband running in place by her side.

The road away from grief is no superhighway. It is, at best, a long drive on an unmarked two-lane road across a vast landscape that you have never before traveled. With each sharp turn in the road, you're as likely to run up against perilous washouts or brakeless trucks crossing into your lane as to watch in despair as the asphalt suddenly grants your wishes for smooth passage and straightens itself out across a seemingly desolate and endless expanse of sand and sage. To stop is to be forever a visitor in someone else's hometown. To keep going means that you must keep your foot on the pedal and your eyes on the road, no matter how tired or scared you might be, until you come upon the exact place on this earth where you know (better than anyone else) you have always belonged, even before the journey began.

Sometimes I wonder if I would have crumbled like the steel cage of car hitting a tree. Or laid down on the side of the road and given up. Or just crawled away like a baby.

But not Patti. She is resilient. She has moxie. She withstood the silent, uncomfortable flight to New Orleans; the agonizing hours full of remorse and condolence leading up to the funeral; the graveside service in Metairie; her sister cradling her newborn baby Isabel; Patti was so big with child that she had to stand with her hand in the small of her back.

And then my young wife leaned into the cold wind on that hot day in Louisiana and strode right back into life. She returned motherless to our cottage on a lake in Wisconsin. She painted the crib, attached a musical mobile from the headboard, hung pastel pictures on the freshly painted walls, sewed delicate cotton infant day shirts, folded the tiny doll diapers, sat quietly by the dock, and waited.

And on July 17, 1969, after more than ten hours of hard labor, the back of her neck soaked with sweat, my fingers crushed in her fist, she pushed and pushed and pushed and pushed for two more agonizing hours until she pushed and pushed our baby boy right on through to the other side.

Cael's birth remains in my memory as the most amazing show of strength and courage—and resilience—I have ever witnessed in my life. From all that I know today, I understand that Patti persevered for herself. She persevered for her mother. She persevered for me. But mostly she did it for her Cael—and the six babies who would follow him into our blessed lives.

And that's what all parents need to do for their kids. To be resilient. So that those who follow us will know resilience in their skin and in their blood and in their bones. So that our children will be able to break on through to the other side when, despite all our beautiful plans and dreams, we can no longer be present and resilient for them.

Rib-Tickling:
The Value of Giggling in a Serious World

> A laugh's the wisest, easiest answer to all that's queer.
>
> —Herman Melville,
> *Moby Dick*

The local Appetite Control meetings used to be held in the basement of the New Paltz Reformed Church. Pausing at the doorway, you would see wooden chairs in neat rows leading up to the inspirational speaker's rostrum and, further back, the impressive multicolored charts and graphs used to illustrate their most up-to-date nutritional plans, guaranteed to taste good, fulfill all dietary requirements, fill you up, *and* allow you to lose the recommended two pounds per week. That is, if you didn't cheat.

And cheating, as every new member was made to understand, was a major sin in this spartan basement. Losing weight was serious business. Your sense of style, your self-esteem, your work life, your sex life, your very existence was dependent upon your will and your ability to choose the correct foods. No fat jokes at the meetings. No finger foods. No cookies. No roly-poly jolly fat people walking around saying it's really okay to slip up every once in a while. No going to the diner after the meeting for a cup of coffee and a Danish. It was all about sticking to the nonstick plan and losing that weight. No funny business. And no cheating.

And short of a serendipitous bout with intestinal flu after an unscheduled feeding frenzy, it was virtually impossible to cheat on the diet and get away with it. The first thing every appetite controller had to do when arriving at a weekly meeting was to weigh in with the dietary counselors. If your fingers just happened to have inadvertently slipped off the cottage cheese tub and mistakenly pulled some mouth-watering wedges of the cherry cheesecake out of the refrigerator on a few occasions that week, those two extra pounds of dessert would certainly betray you at the next meeting.

Which is exactly what fueled Patti's anxiety as she drove into town that night to weigh in. She had been a bad girl that week: a pound or so of butter hidden in the mashed potatoes at Sunday dinner, seconds on the ham, thirds on Monday's red beans and rice made with the sinful ham bone, four well-buttered rolls with dinner by Tuesday night alone, and no less than five bowls of Breyer's French Vanilla (two with devilish hot fudge sauce, but who's counting?) to wash it all down through Wednesday. She knew that the fact that she starved herself all day Thursday would have a meager effect on her official weigh-in Thursday night, but she did it anyway.

Patti had joined the group to help her lose some of the weight she had gained during her pregnancy with Clover. Although she was not heavy in the Roseanne sense of the word, after four children, the few extra pounds she didn't lose at the birth were harder to shed than ever before. So she enlisted in what she indelicately called the Fat Club.

And for two weeks she was a stellar convert to the faith, calculating the fat content of everything she ingested, weighing portions of each meal, denying herself all snacks, refusing butter and sugar and salt, abstaining even from diet desserts. As a measure of her devotion to the AC ideal, this daughter of the Louisiana bayou even went cold turkey on mayonnaise. She was amazing. In fact, she was so good that she lost six pounds in two weeks and was just six more pounds away from her target weight.

But, as many of us learned behind the backs of our kindergarten teachers, being perfectly good is a prelude to being absolutely bad. No one can be that good for long. And, as I mentioned, week three was truly sinful for the virtuous mother of my children.

So she walked into the church building that evening with a dry mouthful of trepidation. The scale would not lie. Perhaps that's why she was a few minutes late and many of the group were already seated in their wooden chairs. She weighed in at plus two pounds, accepted the silent scowls of her nutrition counselor with grace, quietly made her way over to a chair in the back, took off her coat, and, without calling attention to herself, sat down.

And promptly fell to the linoleum floor as the wooden chair cracked, collapsed, and splintered loudly around her!

The hush that followed that harrowing collapse would rival a funeral mass around an open grave, each mourner silently wailing his or her own grief at the terrible and humbling realities of life itself. Patti sat there in a surprised daze on her bottom, wondering what had happened.

And once she started to giggle, she couldn't stop. It was funny! It was ironic. It was absurd. It was so ridiculous, she would have fallen howling to the floor if she wasn't already there.

She looked all around to share the great joke, but the big basement room was quiet. Some looked down on her with pity in their hearts; others turned away, embarrassed by her searching gaze. Apparently her fellow Appetite Controllers were horrified, first at the loss of dignity they imagined she felt, then presumably at the desperate and pathetic way they thought she handled it: giggling and carrying on as if she wasn't as shat-tered inside as the splintered chair in the aisle.

But still Patti was unfazed. "It's funny!" she giggled even louder, assuming that all one needed to do was to reassure her compatriots that she was all right. That it was all right to laugh. "It's funny," she repeated. "We're at a fat club and I broke the chair! It's hysterical!" Upon which her whole body jiggled in paroxysms of laughter.

Alas, no one even chuckled. No one even spoke to her for the rest of the meeting for fear that she might start weeping uncon-trollably.

Yet, despite the extra poundage she gained that week—and the silent treatment she received for giggling—Patti had a good cackling belly laugh with the family when she got home and went back on her diet, though a little bit more reasonably this time. And six weeks later, she hit her target weight.

My guess, as supported by reams of studies about the lack of success of diets of all kinds, is that almost everyone in the meet-ing room that night eventually gained back all the weight they lost in the program. Not simply because they started eating in excess again, but because they didn't laugh at the wonderful absurdity of my good wife breaking her chair and dropping to the linoleum floor.

And Patti, who knows what's funny when she sees it, kept all the weight off. Or at least until she got pregnant with Danny. And although there were two more babies after that—and fif-teen pounds to lose with each of them—Patti ultimately found a weight that was comfortable and healthy and sexy.

The lesson? Don't take yourself so seriously. It could make you overeat.

S

Sex Education:
The Parent as Ill-fitting Chastity Belt

> You may give them your love but not your
> thoughts, / For they have their own thoughts. /
> You may house their bodies but not their souls, /
> For their souls dwell in the house of tomorrow,
> which you cannot visit, not even in your dreams.
> —Kahlil Gibran,
> *The Prophet*

There is simply no way around it: All parents
have to pedal right into the valley of the shadow
of adolescent sex, whether we like it or not. And
we can't just stop when we get exasperated or
frightened. We must pedal all the way to the other
side because, just like toilet training and the first
day of kindergarten, if it doesn't happen, the little
mood swingers will never grow up and leave us
alone.

When Cael entered puberty—which sounds
sort of like he was bicycling along Springtown
Road and suddenly crossed into the unincorpo-
rated Town of Puberty, instantly sprouting pubic

hair and pumping testosterone—I was all for it. I wrapped my arm around his bony shoulders and welcomed him to the trials and tribulations and responsibilities—and salacious pleasures— of manhood. We went camping, and I told him everything he already knew about sex but had no intention of asking (see *Zen and the Art of Fatherhood*). All was well.

But, as all little children understand, boys are different from girls. And a few years later, when daughter number one, Nancy, pedaled along the road with me, I suddenly caught sight of that same sign for Puberty (just as we passed it!) and in a panic grabbed the brakes and tried to spin the bike to cut her off, catapulting myself over the imaginary handlebars and skidding along the pavement into a muddy ditch.

Worse still, Nancy didn't even notice my desperate maneuver. She just kept riding happily along, ready and eager to experience what awaited her along the road.

I sat in my studio that night staring at old photograph albums. I simply could not believe that my baby girl was actually going to grow up on me. The same beautiful, innocent little angel who would glide on top of my feet as we danced to Willie Nelson's "Someone to Watch Over Me." That one. Hair. Breasts. Boys. She would some day have S-E-X! It was impossible to consider.

It was impossible *not* to consider!

If the devil had driven by and offered to make her eternally twelve, I would have seriously considered taking out a home equity loan on my profoundly compromised soul.

Then Patti walked in and laughed at me. Apparently she was dealing with this particular life passage more gracefully than I. She didn't say much, just reminded me that it wasn't too long ago that we were teenagers ourselves.

Which brought me instantly back to a drizzly, foggy night twenty-some-odd years before, when my high school girlfriend J and I were engaged in our favorite extracurricular activity: making out in the front seat of my Earl Sheib'ed green Ford, parked right in front of her house. (It's still amazing to me how two utterly self-conscious teenagers—who thought that everyone's eyes were always on them—would somehow believe that no one could see them when they were making out in public. Anyway . . .)

We were apparently so busily engaged in our "activities" inside the steamed-up car that we failed to notice the porch lights flicking on and off outside her front door. And it was apparently so steamy and hot inside the car that we didn't have all our clothes on.

I don't know how many times the lights had flicked before I looked up—in gasping horror—and saw Mrs. and Mr. G. in their robes storming toward the dark suburban sidewalk under umbrellas. I could only press my trembling finger against the cool and foggy window, to which J screeched something unspellable and slunk down (as if she could hide). And rather than make all the emergency fashion adjustments before her parents barged into our private lives, J simply locked the doors.

And five seconds later, when her six-foot-three-inch bearish father knocked on the window and snarled, "Get out of there!" J absolutely refused to get out of the steel cage.

It was a real suburban standoff: Mr. and Mrs. G. standing in the rain; J slumped down in the locked and steamy car, paralyzed in fear; the boyfriend trembling at the sight of his girlfriend's six-foot-three-inch father pressed against the window. After a few minutes of failed negotiations, I surreptitiously slipped out the driver's door into the surprisingly cool night, slithering over to the parental figures pressed against J's window. I intended to beg for a little extra time for their daughter to regain her composure—and, of course, to get everything back on in the proper order—when the passenger door suddenly bolted open and the three of us watched wide-eyed and slack-jawed as J raced and hopped her way up the slate path to the well-lit house, holding tightly to everything that was falling down or flying off.

That was one bad night.

Yet it showed me the way—long after J and I parted ways—that I might be more than a roadblock on my own teenagers' paths en route to their own good and bad nights.

Although J's parents might have thought at the time that I was a feral child, I was in fact raised by moral people, not wolves. So, standing there all alone with the means of escape dangling in my mottled hands, I reluctantly decided that it wouldn't be right to just drive away. I would face the music— although I was sure there wasn't going to be any music—with my partner in crime. I swallowed hard and followed right behind the robed parents following J into the house.

I was alone in the kitchen for several agonizing eons when J's mom appeared in the doorway like a wet and frazzled angel of mercy. Although I imagined she would, she didn't kick me. She didn't slap me. She didn't even yell. She calmly explained that Mr. G. was too angry to talk, but that she was able to speak for both of them right then.

I nodded, grateful for small favors.

She said that she understood that intimacy and affection (I don't think she said anything about sex per se) were natural and wonderful aspects of growing into adulthood, but there was a time and a place for everything, and parking on a suburban street at midnight was neither the time nor the place. I just kept nodding the whole time. (I still am.)

She also said that there was no way that a parent could monitor a teenager's life twenty-four hours a day; that J and I already knew what was right—which, after seventeen years of parental, school, and religious moralizing, was repetitively true—although the events of that night suggested we still needed to know that she and Mr. G. were looking out the window for us. Soon enough, she said, shaking her head, we would be in college and completely responsible for ourselves. And in the meantime, J's curfew didn't simply mean being near home, it meant being *in* the house.

I nodded. It was true. It still is. If they had forbidden us to see each other—which I'm sure they considered—our bond would only have been strengthened. We would have found each other in the back alleys and hidden corners of our small-town lives. We would have done what we would have done anyway, but without their unseen support.

I nodded one more time, twenty-two years after Mrs. G. politely showed me the door. No matter how long I pouted up there on the third floor or yelled out the window or tried to slam the door against the inexorable forces of Nature—or in the pimply faces of ungentlemanly callers to follow—Nancy was going to grow up. And grow breasts. And go out with boys. And men. I had no choice in the matter.

So I went downstairs and put my arm around those thin shoulders and cheered that momentous first period, welcoming her into the trials and tribulations and responsibilities and, yes, the salacious pleasures of womanhood. Just as I had done with Cael.

BUT, in giving her the advice that Mrs. G. imparted to me in her kitchen, I also let her know that I would be looking out the window every time she left the house. And that curfew didn't simply mean being near home, it meant being *in* the house.

Self-determination:
Question Authority, Even Your Own

> Time has a way of demonstrating / the most stubborn are the most intelligent.
>
> —Yevgeny Yevtushenko, "A Career"

Addie, all of seventeen and full of her high school self, was going toe-to-toe with the old man about something or other (it never really matters, does it). Although I will steadfastly maintain to my dying breath that I am *not* in any shape or form the least bit stubborn, I was at that particular moment drawing my own symbolic line in the familial sand, refusing to give in to the little five-foot-three-inch know-it-all challenging my wisdom and authority on whatever it might have been at the time. I think it concerned car insurance. In any case, I was dug in. And she, who could flex Atlas-like muscles and grow Grendelian claws at a moment's notice, was apparently dug in just as deeply.

I made a wise and imperial thrust with the sword of paternal authority. (A rather good one, I thought.)

She parried with something very high schoolish: the silent stare, I think, head tilted to the side, the one that says, "Duh."

Chin hardened, I offered up an *ex cathedra* retort of stunning pith and weight.

She responded with another rather adolescent tactic, a forced exhalation, a roll of the eyes, and that teen-model scoop of the hair from one side to the other.

I gritted my teeth.

She sneered.

I drew upon my vast experience as a teacher, deftly utilizing the Socratic method in order to back my obstinate daughter into a corner where her only logical recourse would be to admit I was right.

She explained, somewhat compellingly, how I was dead wrong.

So I summoned up a resounding homemade version of the commanding voice of Charlton Heston in Cecil B. DeMille's *The Ten Commandments:* "I am right because I'm older and I know more than you do!" Thunder and lightning pouring down in fearful sheets on Mt. Lewis.

To which she replied most mightily, "Wrong!"

"No, you are wrong!"

"Right!" Sarcasm dripping from her fangs.

"Yes, of course I'm right!" I sputtered, a little confused by the turnaround.

"Yeah, right. How come you're always right and I'm always wrong?"

At which point I lost my cinematic edge and scowled in a most ordinary dad-like tone, "Adelyn, you are so damn contentious!"

There was a pause. Addie then stood at attention like the cute little second grader she once was up in front of the classroom, a triumphant smirk quivering at the edges of her mouth. "Contentious," she enunciated rather crisply and clearly, "irksomely quarrelsome. Contentious."

Upon which my grossly inflated chest deflated like a balloon as I tried to hold in the peals of laughter already escaping my nearly closed throat. The contentious, obstinate little know-it-all had beaten me. She had real spirit. (As it turned out, she had just learned the definition at her SAT class.)

And so it goes. With teenagers, it seems as if you never win. Sometimes you have to give in and sometimes you simply don't. And sometimes you just get blown out of the water by the absurdity of it all. But perhaps the worst thing that can happen to a parent is to raise a teenager who adheres to every rule, who follows every direction, who listens to everything you say. That's a child who will stay a child forever, one who will be at the mercy of every charlatan, every despot, every devil he or she meets.

I never did tell my contentious daughter at the time, but I realized later that night that I was wrong about the car insurance—or whatever it was that we were arguing about. And also that I was resolutely proud of her for questioning my authority.

In a country where how-to books crowd the top of the best-seller lists and the radio dial crackles all day and night with expert financial consultants, shrinks, doctors, political hacks, and "experts" of all kinds, we're in danger of losing the spirit of self-determination with which each of us is born. The kind that saves us, day in and day out, from the designs of the worst of humankind—the ones who would rob us of our spirit.

So I don't want my children *blindly* following anyone's advice. Not mine. Not their mother's. Not a doctor's. Not a teacher's. Not a minister's. Not a spouse's. Certainly not a politician's. And not even their own irksomely quarrelsome children.

I want them to question authority. In questioning authority of all kinds, they may even learn to question the highest authority of all: their own.

Thanksgiving:
Gratitude on a Platter

Holidays / Have no pity.

—Eugenio Montale,
"Eastbourne"

It's pretty much always the same, year after year, and now, after all these years, decade after decade. Following a morning of broken-record warnings to the kids about not eating too much because "you're gonna get stuffed to the gills later on," Patti and I have either herded the growing family into the faltering VW van and puttered down the New York State Thruway to my in-laws' place in Greenwich Village, singing shamelessly along with Arlo Guthrie's "Alice's Restaurant"—or we've made a panic-attacked attempt to clean the three-story mess of a house before the grandparents and city folks arrive up here in the country, along with whoever else is brave or silly enough to share Thanksgiving with us.

Either way, every year Patti's father and his wife, Louanne—and Louanne's sister Lynn—show up hours before any of the other guests, each time catching the hosts mid-broom, mid-oven, and pre-shower. Patti's sister Leigh, her husband, George, and their three kids, Anne, Isabel and Claude, will arrive an hour after the rest of us have broken into the usual hors d'oeuvres. And any way you slice it, there will be two massive birds; mountains of stuffing and mashed potatoes and sweet potatoes with marshmallows; acres of green beans, peas, and salad; truckloads of cranberries and warm rolls; enough wine, soda, and beer to swill it all down; and, just when everyone is too stuffed to take another bite, a cauldron's worth of coffee and enough pumpkin, mince, and apple pies to send everyone in the family to the local emergency room for a good stomach pumping.

Which of course never happens.

Which of course is predictable. This year, as in years past, my brother-in-law George—painter, sculptor, and designated carver at all family gatherings involving meat—will wonder aloud once again how it has come to pass that he is always the one chosen to slice up the birds; I will smile pleasantly or hold up fingers with Band-Aids to demonstrate beyond any doubt why he must do it; little Elizabeth will show everyone who walks by her homemade turkey centerpiece; Anne's friend Scott and Isabel's friend Lyle (neither of whom have little brothers) will play computer games and floor hockey with Bay (whose older siblings, who do in fact have a little brother, will be watching football on TV); Nancy, Addie, and Clover's boyfriends will show up for their second Thanksgiving meals; and all of them, along with Anne, Isabel, Cael, Claude, and Danny, will be busy gorging themselves on what remains of the mounds of chips and dips in the living room.

And so it will go, as it typically goes in many American homes on the fourth Thursday of every November. Here we will chortle at Paw Paw's annual joke about a fish; we'll groan when Patti and Leigh lead a lame, discordant chorus of "We Gather Together"; we'll eat too much and laugh about it, pants loosened and zippers undone; someone will recall, to the annual great howls of laughter, the time Leigh drank the custard sauce (for the bread pudding) and thought it was eggnog; Patti will say something about making soup with the "corcusses," and her children will fall to the floor in hysterics as if it's the first time they heard her mispronounce the word; George will disappear for hours before someone locates him in the bathroom; and I will fall asleep, mouth open like my father's, who himself will be suffering an overdose of bird on a couch in Florida, mouth dropped open like his son's.

And when Patti and Louanne disappear out onto the porch to sneak a smoke, the rest of us will look around at the leftovers and agree—as we agreed last November—that there will be enough leftovers to last until Christmas, when we will all get together once again to eat until we are ready to pop.

But once again we will be wrong. By the time Leigh and George bend and fold their tall selves the following afternoon into the unbelievably brown Subaru wagon that they perennially claim to be trading in—or we file out of their apartment like clowns out of a VW Beetle—every scrap of food will be ripped from the carcasses, scraped from the bowls, snatched from the pie tins, and chewed and digested. There will be nothing left but mounds of dishes.

Nothing changes. Not the menu. Not the bad jokes. Not the complaints. Not the reminiscences about previous Thanksgiving dinners. Not even the fact that no one thinks to stop and give thanks.

And year after year everyone agrees that it's just simply not worth the weeks of preparation and expense for a single meal. And that it's such a terrible waste at a time when most of the world lives in poverty. And that it's gotten to be so difficult getting everyone together as the kids grow up and have their own lives and families. And that besides, it's so damn unhealthy.

And then we go and do it all over again the next November.

Because Montale was right: Holidays have no pity. They bring you home, with a light hand on the scruff of the neck, and show you exactly who you are and where you come from. Thanksgiving is a valued part of real family life because it exists for no other reason than to show us just how ordinary and cyclical life really is; how much we need each other to laugh at the circles we keep making out of our lives; how life goes on after we move beyond the circles we trace; and how grating and predictable the daily grind might be if we didn't have these celebrations of gratitude to fall back on even as we fail once again to express our gratitude for having all of us around to grace each other's table.

Tradition:
The Annual Hated Love Fest

> There is nothing sacred about convention: there is
> nothing sacred about primitive passions or whims; but
> the fact that a convention exists indicates that a way of
> living has been devised capable of maintaining itself.
> —George Santayana,
> *Persons and Places*

With seven kids in the family, we routinely celebrate no less than nine birthdays a year—as well
as Christmas, Hanukkah, New Year's, July 4th,
Halloween, Thanksgiving, and various anniver-
saries among a host of regularly irregular reverent
and irreverent occasions of no particular note. As
such, there would seem to be no compelling reason to make a big deal out of Valentine's Day, an
annual event that costs too much money and routinely causes more heartache and grief than all the
squishy romantic love it is supposed to create.
(One of the more poignant memories I have of
teaching ninth grade was watching lovely Tara

Rough, wearing a candy corsage and carrying a bouquet of red and white flowers, walking dreamily down the halls of Millbrook High, followed by dozens of weepy, despondent, empty-armed girls.)

Yet somewhere along the well-traveled path of homemade family traditions, the Lewis hordes started making something out of the nothing that is Cupid's big day. As February 14 approaches each year, every disgruntled member of the family points in my annually stunned direction and claims that it's all my fault. (At those moments I take great comfort from radio shrinks like Joy Brown, who remind us daily that we are not responsible for others' unhappiness.)

It all started with the fact that I've never really appreciated the processed slices of cheesy emotion packaged with such floral disingenuousness at greeting card factories. Nor do I understand why a dozen roses is such a magic number—and why a dozen longstems costs $60 at our little upstate flower shop around Valentine's Day, but if it's late and you're desperate, they're only $7.99 at Shop Rite. Also, despite the bright red heartshaped boxes, not one of the mystery chocolates inside is ever as good as a plain Hershey's.

So, one evening around twelve years ago, in a pique of righteousness against the evils of Mass Production and the Industrial Revolution and Conspicuous Consumption, I merely suggested to the family slouching around the living room that we *make*—not buy—Valentine's cards. That woke them up. Cael nearly choked. "You mean, construction paper, scissors, markers, magazines, glitter, glue, doilies?"

Yes.

"Like arts and c-c-crafts at Camp Chinqueka?" stuttered Nancy in a panic.

Yes.

"Me too?" gasped my good wife, who is busy enough without having to be Martha Stewart.

In retrospect, I'm amazed that no one had the presence of mind to tell me that I was welcome to make Valentine's cards if I'd like, but they were perfectly happy buying their sentiments at Dedricks Pharmacy in town. A few days later, the long pine table resembled an art room in an elementary school. There were scraps of paper all over the blue Oriental rug, globs of glue on fingers and chairs, cuffs and collars permanently stained with indelible markers, and tears of frustration from little ones who envisioned art-directed Hallmark precision and got kindergarten-primitive cute.

There were two unanticipated consequences of going cold-Hallmark: one, that everyone actually seemed to have a good time creating original if terribly bizarre homemade master-pieces that spoke of love yet chided siblings and parents alike for their characteristic faults; and two, that all the older kids—and of course Patti and me—found a peculiar motivation in trying to outdo everyone else by making the best-designed and funniest cards in the family. Cutthroat family competition being what it is, Nancy, Addie, and I stayed up long past midnight on that first February 13 in order to impress our stubbornly unimpressible relatives. (Although we didn't have a formal awards ceremony, I'm certain that I would have won the Cupid for Outstanding Art Direction of a Situation-Comedy Card.) And Valentine's Day dinner, complete with a pastel-iced cake in the shape of a lamb, was a big hit. Glittery, gaudy cards and uneaten cake scattered all over the kitchen, I smirked my smug pleasure over my doubting family.

Then came Valentine's Day II. Encouraged by the rousing success of VD I, I raced home from the local art supplies store and ceremoniously dumped all the exciting new crafts materials on the kitchen table. Six-year-old Danny cheered. The rest looked at me as if I was the proprietor of the Bates Motel. I believe it was Nancy who said, "You mean we have to do this all over again? I thought last year was it."

"Of course we do," I smiled uneasily. The silence was not at all deafening, as some writers like to imagine. It was utterly noiseless.

"Can't we just give each other last year's cards?" Cael suggested.

"No," I growled, and pushed the packages of multicolored

construction paper around the table and set up the glue, scissors, markers, glitter, and doilies. "Besides, I already bought all this stuff. Now make the damn Valentine's cards!"

Of course everyone got into the spirit, laughing at each other, crumbling up botched ideas and throwing them at me, arguing over possession of black and red magic markers, and of course checking to see who was making the best and most ridiculous cards. (Once again, I'm sure I did.)

And after the overwhelming success of VD II, I once again assumed that the family would look forward to III with great enthusiasm. And once again I was wrong. Patti actually snarled at me, with a pack of child-like wolves circling behind her. All those glistening fangs convinced me that it was time to surrender to the New Age.

Unfortunately, the construction paper and glitter monster already had a life of its own. Danny and Clover, who would spend a sum total of four and half minutes making their six Valentine's cards apiece, loved getting those wonderfully funny and creative cards that would take the rest of us four and a half days to construct. They demanded that the tradition go on. "Besides," said Clover, "it's Bay's first Valentine's Day, and we just can't stop now." And three years later, when Elizabeth showed up for number VI, it seemed we were super-glued to the annual custom.

New Age Valentine's Day number XIII is soon upon us. Like Frankenstein's homemade monster, it is by now completely beyond my control. Except for Elizabeth and Bay, who are still too young to understand the can of gummy worms that I opened twelve years ago, everyone else begins the dreaded countdown to Valentine's Day right after the equally tiresome yearly Super Bowl party.

The tradition should end here and now. But the annual hated lovefest is so woven into the fabric of our lives that to abandon the loathsome arts and crafts—and return to the packaged sentiments at Hallmark—would be like removing a day from the year.

Family traditions—from the roadside diner you always stop

at on the way to the beach to the annual celebration of the wedding of the two people who fell in love and created the family in the first place—are the ways in which we learn to value our remarkably short time on earth together. As Patti and I have seen, a family's year passes more quickly than a camcorder in the hands of a child sweeping across a back yard birthday party. If we don't stop and celebrate the great and the small, the joyous and the annoying, the sacred and the profane, it will all be just a blur on the TV screen.

Usefulness:
Reflections on One's Mother and the Dalai Lama

> A useless life is early death.
>
> —Goethe,
> *Iphigenia in Taurus*

When asked by a reporter about whether he would be interested in future genetic therapies that will allow people to live much longer lives, the exalted Dalai Lama answered, "The mere living is not so important. The important thing is usefulness" (*New York Times Magazine*, September 29, 1996).

I stopped myself right then and there from turning the page and getting absorbed in something as pointless as the Sunday crossword puzzle. It takes the stunning mindfulness of a Dalai Lama to remind us that if we are not actually contributing to the quality of existence on earth, then we cease to grow as individuals or as a people. We become hollow men and women.

Then I tried the crossword. And failed.

As a survivor of the toxic "me first and me only" environs of sub-urban Long Island (pronounced Lawn Guylind), New Yawk, where I grew up—or perhaps down—I bear witness to the deplorable waste of existence via obedience to the gods of cashmere, carats, and Cadillac Coup de Villes. Spiritual death sprawled all around me at a very early age. The neighborhood was overpopulated with early adherents to Billy Crystal's Fernando and his flourish to earthly wisdom, "It's better to look good than feel good."

Ever since those salad days on Lawn Guylind were over—and Patti and I started serving up side salads to our own little carnivores—I've thought a great deal about the meaning of a well-lived life. I've spent countless hours driving home from long days in the classroom wondering whether an ordinary man with nothing more than an ordinary talent for teaching and writing contributes anything of value to the universe in his lifetime. Despite my decidedly commonplace dreams, I am no John Dewey or Bill Shakespeare, whose ideas cast a light and a spell on individuals and nations.

And then, literally thousands of times over, I have walked across the cluttered mudroom floor and through the kitchen door of a warm home filled with good children whose lives are so profoundly affected by the unerring presence of their extra-ordinary mother. And I wonder if usefulness should be seen in far less public terms.

The other day I found a note underneath a chair in the living room that Elizabeth had written to Patti. The orange paper was folded six times the long way and twice the short way; and whether it matters or not, had I not found it, I'm sure Patti probably never would have seen it. In her inimitable scrawl (pencil held between the third and fourth fingers despite all the adult pressure to do it "right"), Elizabeth wrote:

Dear Mama,

I love you, you are my favrit person in the wrld.

I love you, Elizabeth

Of course, I welled up. Not only because it was so pure and sweet and fragile, but because, like the Dalai Lama, it so simply answered all my questions. Patti has devoted her life to that little girl—and her brothers and sisters—in a most elegant and purposeful way. And no one knows it or commends it more than Elizabeth herself. Yes, Usefulness is a profoundly private matter. And parenthood is perhaps the most pristine example of it. Even back on Lawn Guylind, where my friends' mothers, despite outlandish taste in clothes and jewelry and cars, were loving and dutiful parents.

And so, of course, I thought about my own mother. At the risk of sounding like a mama's boy à la Richard Nixon or Jimmy Carter or Bill Clinton, each of whom utilized his mother to his best advantage to gain the national *Aw, he loves his mother* vote, my mother quietly emerges—like the message on an eight ball—as the manifestation of the Dalai Lama's—and Elizabeth's—timeless pronouncement. Neither rich nor famous, she didn't write books or lecture at Harvard or drag people out of burning buildings or preside over a board of any shape or size—or even produce children of great fame or fortune. She didn't work "outside the home," as the politically correct phrases the non-politically correct "she never had any gainful employment" (meaning of course that she never made any *real* money). Yet, like many women of her era, she not only fulfilled a biological destiny by birthing and nurturing three children to no fanfare, she painted and sculpted without making a single sale; she was Cub Scout den mother for free; a literacy/Head Start volunteer with no plaque to show for her efforts; a uniquely good person who has cooked and dusted and knitted hundreds of sweaters and quietly cheered on her children's and grandchildren's and great-grandchildren's best efforts without a single mention in the news. A woman shimmering with generations and generations of purposeful life.

I remember once fidgeting my way through a biblically long discussion on "The Well-Lived Life" at a local Unitarian church, thinking that this was the most purposeless and wasteful two hours I'd spent in all my years. So if I may be succinct—

and as presumptuous as to speak for the Dalai Lama, Bill Shakespeare, and Johann Goethe—the ol' boys and I salute my mother and all the other good parents who don't need to waste precious time pondering the obvious.

Uselessness
Is Also Nice

> A man cannot sleep in his cradle; whatever is useful in the nature of life must become useless.
> —Walter Lippmann,
> *A Preface to Politics*

I know, I know, I know. You probably just read my inspired homage to useful living—and motherhood and the Dalai Lama—and this looks like it's going to contradict everything I said. Well, as Uncle Walt Whitman wrote, "Do I contradict myself? / Very well then I contradict myself, / (I am large, I contain multitudes)." Contradiction is the backbone of real family living, because as anyone who has ever shared living space with a teenager knows, what is undeniably true one second cannot be counted on to be true the next.

Yes, purposeful living is to be admired. BUT, as one who still has a teenager just hangin' out behind the crow's feet around his eyes, I'm painfully aware that grinding utilitarianism is nothing short

of boring, mundane, predictable, rigid. Rigor mortised. A but-
terfly under glass. From Goethe, who must have been quite a
laid-back guy himself, "Complete usefulness is death."

So how does one reconcile the value of function and order in
the family with the natural yearning to stay in bed and do
absolutely nothing worthwhile? Why just sit down in the face
of everything and everyone (parents, teachers, clergy, bosses,
bank tellers, public address announcers, etc.) who tell you to
get up and do something?

Because, as Bill Murray exhorts his lame, dweeby campers in
the non-award-winning movie *Meatballs*, "It just doesn't matter." It simply does not matter.

Take one simple step back from your life—sit down for a
moment and picture yourself in a hospice bed or a car about to
crash head-on into a brick wall—and you'll see very clearly
that the well-ordered life, the extra hours at work, the perfect
lawn, the flawless diamond, the dustless house, the corner
office, the winning goal, the trophy on the mantel—all of it—
are not nearly as valuable as you thought at the time. And it all
pales dreadfully in comparison with the moments of pure
unadulterated laughter and companionship that happened for
no good reason at all. My dearest times with Patti and the kids
have never been the big vacations or those momentous
moments that do not pass without a donation to Kodak.
They've simply been the scattered moments of walking aim-
lessly in the woods or the city, giggling pointlessly at something I couldn't begin to explain why it was funny, loving each
of them in the moment for no good reason other than it felt so
good to be in love.

I used to show that clip from *Meatballs* to my overly stressed
Advanced Placement English students on the last class before
their predictably harrowing three-hour AP exam. A few of the
kids who had been listening with their inner ears to the way I
stumbled through the curriculum all year suddenly smiled as if
they finally understood what I'd been trying to tell them since
the previous September. Most of the others, however, looked at
me as if I'd just lost my shaky grip on reality.

"You're kidding," said one A student who had done all the work masterfully but never heard the voices of the writers in their books.

"I'm not kidding," I smiled, hoping to nudge her into the contemplation of nothingness.

"You mean all the work that we've done this year leading up to this horrible exam is worthless?"

"Oh no, not at all. The work that brought you to this point, to this question, is good. It's the test itself that is worthless."

"It's worth up to six college credits," she challenged, eyes crumbled together like tin foil. "That's not nothing."

"No, but it still doesn't matter. You'll be the same person whether you get a one [the lowest score] or a five [the highest]. Everyone who loves you will still love you. Everyone who hates you will still hate you. You're going to look the same, walk the same, feel the same. A few credits more or less will not alter the direction of your life. Achievement is an illusion. In the end, nobody wins—and, because nobody wins, nobody loses."

She looked at me as if I was a complete and total loser.

That's all right. I learned a lot about dedication and stick-to-it-tive-ness from her that year. That's just as important as having a little Teflon in your life. I only hope she gained some measure of the value of uselessness from me. Balance is everything.

Of all my children, Clover is probably the one who best understands the *Meatballs* philosophy of life. Clover could lie in a hammock or float in the ocean all day long. *All* day long. As a person who understands the illusory nature of achievement, she is unbounded by personal ambition. She is a pure spirit who grudgingly accommodates the world of reason and purpose.

Which is why I won't show her this chapter, but I will stick the one on Usefulness under her pillow.

V

Virtue:
The Virtue of Keeping One's Virtue to Oneself

> If a man has no vices, he's in great danger of making vices about his virtues, and there's a spectacle.
> —Thornton Wilder,
> *The Matchmaker*

Take a drive along historic Route 66 or the now infamous Santa Monica Freeway or just make a right and head on over to the mall—it doesn't really matter—you're bound to see a bold variation on that self-congratulatory bumper sticker cruising down the endless American road: MY CHILD IS AN HONOR STUDENT AT . . . From Oregon to Delaware, prideful parents of B+ students are doing the same in-your-face bumper macarena for their fellow motorists stuck behind them in traffic.

I understand in the very muscles of my face the sense of pride that all parents feel in their kids' achievements. And I'm aware that children feel "validated," as the pop psychologism goes, by Mom's and Dad's unabashed boastings after their kids have done something good—or well. But from the vantage point of having known hundreds, perhaps even thousands, of teenagers who are painfully embarrassed to be seen driving in the same car with their parents, it is also acne-clear that most teenagers would rather attend a yearlong series of lectures on The Virtuous Teenage Life than see that particular bumper sticker affixed to a car in which they are riding.

And why would it be preferable for teenagers to have to listen to some pasty-faced adult drone on and on, week after week, rather than see such a public expression of their parents' pride? The answer is quite simple: Most kids are not nearly as disingenuous as adults.

Kids know exactly what the bumper sticker is all about. They know it's not just about pride. Pride is a smile, a hug, a tear, a cracked voice, a quiet word at the end of the day, an unexpected whoop from the packed crowd at the basketball game. The bumper sticker is the athletically challenged form of chest-bumping in the NBA or end zone dancing in the NFL. It says, in the plainest of American idioms, MY KID IS BETTER THAN YOUR KID or, better still, NA NA NA NA NA NA. Kids think it's snobby. They know it's meant to put someone else down. As I mentioned earlier, accusing teenagers of being *conceited* is probably the second worst slur you can fling in their faces—right after *dumb*—and both of those qualities are handily addressed by that one supposedly innocent bumper sticker.

Besides, is there anything more lip-chewing annoying than having to listen to some parent bragging about his or her child, especially if your own children are majoring in detention? In practically any group there is a mom or dad who thinks that everyone in town is sitting at the edge of their bleacher seats waiting to hear about Artie's A or Beatrice's acceptance to Barnard or Carley's deep spiritual commitment to the homeless in Scarsdale. It happens on line in the A&P, standing on the sidelines at a soccer game, in those generic family Christmas "letters." I figure you shouldn't have to deal with it in rush-hour traffic.

As Danny told me recently (did I tell you that Danny was elected president of . . . no, forget it), there are only two reasonable responses to seeing that message sticking its tongue out at you on the highway: 1) It makes parents of non-honor roll students feel like *losers* and 2) It dares even the most laid-back of teenagers to just pop the clutch and roll right into the bumper sticker of the insulting car when they've stopped behind it at a light.

Despite the best wishes of school administrators, it's pretty clear that the ubiquitous honor roll bumper sticker simply does not—and will not—inspire any other parent to encourage any teenager to enjoy school more, spend more time on homework, or listen more intently in class. And it does not—and will not—move a single adolescent boy or girl to work harder or study longer in order to glue that particular phrase on the family car.

Similar in effect to all those hopeful fabrications our parents' generation told us about *walking ten miles to school each morning*, the net result, then, is just as most kids would be able to predict it is: Zero for children. A bundle for the bumper sticker industry. And little or nothing for the parent or the school board member who initiated the program. Yet it takes up considerable space on the crowded bumpers of life.

Like most forms of self-righteousness, it produces little more than the three Dark Rs of Family Values: Rejection, Resentment, and Remorse. The very children we hope to touch with the message reject it for what it is; they resent the hypocritical manipulation that any teenager can read in between the lines; and, worst of all, they feel remorse at not being good enough or smart enough or trustworthy enough to be trusted with the truth.

Virtue is good. True virtue reflects moral excellence. I recommend it for everyone, especially everyone in my family. But when wearing virtue like some kind of public badge of honor with noses tipped high above the speeding traffic, we should all be very careful not to lose sight of the winding road and veer off into a ditch, bumper up in the air. None but the truly virtuous will stop to help us.

Vice:
By Any Other Name Is No Virtue

> I was never so rapid in my virtue but my vice kept up with me.
>
> —Henry David Thoreau,
> *Journal*

I wasn't feeling particularly virtuous when I woke to another day of rain, despite the fact that all I had ahead of me was a long and soul-cleansing list of dad chores. New in town and essentially friendless, Patti, Cael, baby Nancy, and I were just finding how gray and cold and isolated a beautiful New England fall could become. The charming 200-year-old house nestled under massive firy-colored maples in October 1973 was fast turning into a breezeway for the cold winds sluicing down the mountain in November. And those lovely red and gold leaves were no longer riffling in the crisp apple-scented wind, but laying on the wet muddy ground, suffocating an acre of green grass. I felt just as cold and stymied as the poor flattened grass.

Four-year-old Cael and I were doing the universal manly breakfast thing of slurping up cereal while listlessly staring at whatever was right in front of us; he was totally absorbed by the box of corn flakes, and I was reading Craig McKinney's local weekly, *The New Paltz News*. Having moved to New Paltz from Wisconsin just a month before, I didn't recognize one name in the entire thirty-two-page paper.

Out of the dim stupor of Saturday breakfast, though, Cael wondered aloud what fun things we were doing that day. And as I was not feeling particularly generous, I grumbled out a daunting list of weekend chores ranging from the sublime pleasure of going to the dump to the laugh-a-minute fun of changing the ball cock in the toilet. When he whined that it all sounded boring—and how cold it was in the kitchen—I groused, "Well, life isn't always fun. And today is just one of those days."

Cael went back to the box of corn flakes that he couldn't read, his lower lip shading his wet chin, and my lower lip inadvertently aping his. But I perked up immediately when my wandering eyes landed on a small ad for *Cinderella*, which was playing in Highland, a Hudson River town just a few miles away. Well, not *Cinderella* precisely, but obviously a new version called *Cinderella Goes Around the World*.

"Virtue be damned!" a voice whispered from inside my right ear. It sounded remarkably like my old carousing buddy Jim Hazard from Wisconsin.

"Take care of your responsibilities like a man!" my deeply embedded father groused in my left ear.

But there was to be no Jiminy Cricket debate over conscience that morning. Knowing that I could avoid the boring chores and still look virtuous by taking my son to a matinee— and maybe even meet some other young parents along the way—the Jim Hazard voice slapped me on the back and the world suddenly began to warm up. By noon, as I bundled Cael up in his best upstate mock-hunting gear, I was feeling downright generous. We were going to see a fun movie, eat popcorn and Twizzlers, and meet some interesting people.

And not do what we were supposed to do. A dad's life doesn't get much better than that.

The theater, located on narrow Vineyard Avenue in the little hamlet, was called an Art Cinema. It was certainly unusual to see an arty movie house showing cartoons, but I assumed that the Fellini, Buñuel, and Bergman types were simply making a reluctant bow to the bottom line by filling some seats for a Saturday matinee. I didn't much care; my little pal and I were off to the movies with my virtue intact—and I was not standing in the rain trying to dump heavy metal barrels into the smelly landfill.

I was very surprised, though, as we racewalked up to the theater and didn't see a snaking line of parents and toddlers going around the corner, like we used to find at every Saturday matinee at the Downer Theater back in Milwaukee (where we also virtuously avoided our chores). In fact, there was nobody standing under the small marquee, which now only advertised part of the title, *Cinderella Goes Around.*

A big, stupid grin skittered across my face as we skidded up to find an old lady sitting alone in the even older ticket booth. She wore a heavy winter jacket that looked like it had once belonged to a teenager and was smoking an unfiltered cigarette.

"Did it already start?" I panted.

She shook her head, the cigarette dangling from her thin lips. She peered over the edge. "Is he coming in?"

I tilted my head like a confused labrador retriever. "Yeah, of course."

She shrugged. "That'll be five dollars," the blue smoke stuttering out between syllables. I slid a five under the glass and Cael and I racewalked into the lobby. Both of us stopped short, mouths open, in front of the dark, uninhabited candy counter.

"How could they show a kids' movie and not sell popcorn?" I muttered, seriously wondering if we had moved to a region of ignorant child haters. There was a candy machine in the corner, though, and two quarters and five yanks later we had a brick-hard Snickers and a water-stained packet of M&M's in hand.

The musty theater was nearly empty when we pushed back

the curtains and made our way down the aisle, a few single men scattered around in dark brown Naugahyde seats. Not one turned to look as we found excellent seats in the exact middle of the middle row.

"This is very, very cool," I said to little Cael as I handed him the M&M's. "We must be really early." He shrugged; he didn't care, his stubby digits ripping open the candy.

But then the lights dimmed even further and the projector popped and sizzled and chintzy music sputtered out of the speakers as the full title, *Cinderella Goes Around The World*, moved like a snake around a globe, disappearing as the camera panned in on the earth first, then North America, then New York City, then a nondescript apartment building, then a metal casement window, and then four shoes lined up on a rug: two women's high heels on either end facing the camera and two men's loafers facing the bed, which slowly comes into view as the camera moves up to the mattress, exposing four bare feet in similar arrangement.

By the time the camera slowly zoomed up the four bare legs and reached a big naked hairy butt, I had Cael's head stuffed in my coat and we were stumbling out of the empty row and making a beeline toward the ticket booth. I was steamed, set to bellow and scream and rant and rave and threaten letters to *The New Paltz News*, not to mention lawsuits and the wrath of God—and of course to demand my money back—when I found the booth as dark and empty and locked as the candy counter. I knocked on the glass and yelled out, "Hey! I want my money back!"

The old lady reappeared in a haze of smoke, a smirk snickering at the edge of her thin lips. She pushed a wrinkled five back under the glass.

By then Cael had wriggled his little mophead out of the coat and whined, "Why can't we watch the movie, Daddy? I didn't get to see anything."

"Good," I said with the great relief that there was nothing to explain. "I'm really sorry, Caely. This just isn't a movie for little boys." And when I turned back to give the old lady my two cents' worth, she was gone.

"Well," I hugged my disappointed boy, "how 'bout we go over to Ed's for some ice cream?"

"I don't wanna. I wanna watch a movie, I wanna watch a movie, I wanna watch a moo-oo-oovie!!!!" He was bawling as we stood out on the sidewalk, cold wind and rain driving us back to the car—and home—and the dump—and the damn toilet.

What's the moral? You can't cover a smelly vice with sweet-smelling virtue. The stink comes through. As Shakespeare's *King Lear* reminds us, "The gods are just, and of our pleasant vices / Make instruments to scourge us."

Work:

Chores as a Form of Grace

> Work spares us from three great evils: boredom, vice, and need.
>
> —Voltaire,
> *Candide*

Laid out on the couch with cabin fever *in extremis,* I was channel-surfing on the TV and trying to figure out whether I should wake Danny to help me shovel the seven feet of snow off the roof of the front porch when one of those spine-tingling Sunday golf tournaments appeared on the screen. I opened my eyes wide, suddenly mesmerized by the long green fairways, the lighter green thick roughs, the lusciously deep green greens. Grass.

A few minutes later, for reasons still not clear to me, I was climbing over a five-foot mound of plowed snow to get into the barn. Perhaps because I hadn't seen the lawn since Christmas, it seemed terribly important at the moment to get to the old John Deere. I sat on the hard dusty seat. Wrapped my fingers around the cold steering wheel. Pushed down the frozen clutch.

When T. S. Eliot wrote, "April is the cruelest month," I'm pretty sure he wasn't considering the frozen solid end of February or early March, and certainly not about sitting on a rusty old riding mower. Yet looking out over the crusty snow covering just about everything in sight, and imagining the soggy bedraggled spring lawn underneath it all, I could see Eliot's point. Sapped by another harsh winter, in the advent of spring one might feel a certain hopelessness at the endless cycle of seasons leading everywhere and nowhere at the same time. There's no escaping the fact that each moment of renewal also signals a new round in the futile struggle to gain a step on time. And despite our best efforts to keep our perilous existences neat and mowed and under control, the second hand keeps sweeping, and the grass keeps growing.

Every spring since 1973 in this remarkable green region, I have urged myself to plod out to the barn to begin the process anew. Nihilistic despair aside, it doesn't take a brain surgeon to know that if I don't cut the grass, I won't have a lawn. As a hayfield it may look very pretty, but the snakes and deer ticks that come to live there would make my family's life miserable and perilous. So I mow.

The dilemma—or the truly cruel part for me—is that when I have finally cranked up enough energy to attack spring before its glory is literally scratching at my knees, the obstinate mower never works: the battery is dead, or a belt needs replacing, or a tire is flat, or it needs a new plug or a clean air filter—take your pick, it is *always* something. As the engine whines and wheezes and coughs and backfires black smoke into the cold fresh air, I sit there on the dusty seat, looking out over the mocking green over the septic tank, wondering what I've done once again to deserve my fate.

So, on that cold and windy winter afternoon, looking beyond the crusty snow to the unrelenting lawn I would have to mow at least through the following October, I resigned myself to my destiny and turned the cold ignition.

Of course it didn't start, whining and whining like my kids on the three or four days they actually went to school in February, and then sputtering into a cold mechanical silence. I hate mowing. At that precise moment of despair, I was sorely tempted to sell the machine and call up my friend Frank Ciliberto, a local teacher who also has a lawn care business.

Hiring Frank would not be a bad idea when one considers things like cost-effectiveness and the value of leisure time. My time and energies could be better used than by fixing, riding, riding, and fixing an obstinate lawn tractor all spring, summer, and fall. Considering mounting repair costs and the price of a new tractor (which costs more than my first three cars combined), I could probably have my lawn maintained for eight to ten years, or the time it would take to render another machine aggravatingly useless.

All those hours would be mine to spend "quality time" with my family, or to make a few extra bucks, or just to relax in the Adirondack chair with a good book while I hear the hum of someone else doing my work.

As soon as I convinced myself to go inside and give Frank a call, I started getting sentimental about odd things like my father's first motorized push mower, a stupid-looking contraption that never worked, or riding around the lawn with toddlers in my lap, or teaching each succeeding twelve-year-old how to handle the beast of a machine. And from there I could almost smell the sweet grass in the moment that it is cut, the sun on my bare back, my mind wandering beyond the breezy treeline, sweat pouring down my chest, and, dues paid, the extraordinary sensation of sinking into the Nags Head hammock strung between two white pines, a cold Corona in my still-quivering hand, gazing out at the elegant beauty of a simple job well done. And suddenly there was nothing in the world I wanted to do more than mow the lawn.

So there I sat, slumping in near despair on the cold-as-ice John Deere, a mass of tangled contradictions. I hate mowing. I love mowing. Sometimes it's this way; sometimes it's that way; and sometimes it's simply nowhere to be found.

So when I began to shiver uncontrollably, as if I were just a few minutes from a hypothermic stupor, ventricular fibrillation, and early death, I came to the conclusion that there could be worse things than mowing a lawn. To be blunt, each instant of delight and frustration is available to every one of us on a painfully limited basis as we move along toward old age and death. As Thornton Wilder reminds us in *Our Town*, "One man in ten thinks it's a privilege to push his own lawn mower." Or to teach his children the value of mowing the lawn. Or to just sit on a green John Deere in the barn, I might add.

So I climbed off the green beast, stumbled over the mound of plowed snow and walked back into the warm house to wake up Danny from his long winter yawn—and the two of us manhandled the porch roof. My arms aching, my neck sweating, I stood on the porch roof looking ahead to another cruel spring of mower breakdowns, one more hot and itchy summer of mowing malaise, and a fall wrought with mower and mowee collapse, just like the last. And along the way I made plans to love every miserable moment that's available to me. Amen.

Wisdom:
Knowing Who You Are

> The questions which one asks oneself begin, at last,
> to illuminate the world, and become one's key to
> the experience of others.
>
> —James Baldwin,
> *Nobody Knows My Name*

Twice assured that I had on clean underwear and matching white socks, my mother checked my fingernails. We were going to buy a suit for my bar mitzvah. My first suit.

As we drove through the maze of neat ranch houses and pedicured lawns in our suburban development, I tried to describe the "Philip Gaynor Look" to my mother, but she just shook her head in exasperated confusion. Philip Gaynor, for the uninformed, was my best friend's older brother, a junior in high school.

As we entered the dark, cool Eliot Store, my mother put her hand on my scrawny neck and ushered me to the back near the dressing rooms. She knew what she was doing. And when she pointed out the five dark suits from which I was supposed to choose, my heart sank. They all looked like suits my father would have worn. I shrugged, close to tears.

And when the salesman hurried over, baggy pants flopping over his brown shoes, my mother said, "Try one on, just for size—"

The salesman concurred, "—just for size. You don't have to get it."

I was old enough to know what they were doing, but too young to stop it. As I silently agreed to their conspiratorial plan, I knew that I would end up with the very same suit I tried on. I settled for the least offensive one on the rack. My mother said it was charcoal gray.

The salesman held out the jacket like a matador holds a cape. As soon as I was locked in, he jerked down the back, walked around to the front, and tugged at the lapels, then the sleeves, then buttoned all three buttons despite my protestations that I would never button my jacket. Philip Gaynor never did.

"Perfect!" he exclaimed to my mother. I was then handed the slacks and ordered into the changing room while the tailor was found. The slacks were two feet too long, baggier than my pajamas, and the crotch was located somewhere near my knees.

I padded out of the dressing room with a wad of gray material bunched around my white socks, a silly grin on my face as I waited for the howls of laughter.

"Gudt!" spat out the short, balding tailor with pins between his shadowy lips. He also wore baggy pants; his sleeves were rolled and his tie loosened. I turned to my mother with a smirk. She avoided my eyes. He said, "Get up there," pointing to the carpeted riser.

He shook his head for no reason that I could figure out, put his stubby fingers through the belt loops near my hips, and hiked the pants up just below my nipples. "Dat's not vere a man vears his pants, sonny—on your vaist!"

I thought my waist was down on my hips like it was on all boys. "But I don't—"

"You'll vear 'em dere," he said sternly, giving one more tug on the belt loops. Again I looked to my mother, but she was not going to save me.

Next, he pulled out a yellow tape measure, stuck one end just beneath my scrotum, and slid the other hand down along the tape to my ankle. Shrinking into myself, I stifled a giggle that normally would have sent me crumbling to the floor in hysterics. "Straighten up, sonny!" he yelled. I straightened up.

It was bad enough that the man was touching me there, but he kept saying the word "crotch" right in front of my mother. I didn't even know whether she had ever heard that word before. But the final indignity came when, realizing that my dream of being the next Philip Gaynor was turning into a nightmare, I said meekly that I wanted thirteen-inch cuffs.

"No!" came the disgusted reply. "Dese aren't dunkarees, sonny. You vant to be a man, dress like a man!"

After he solemnly put his hieroglyphics on the suit with a thin sliver of chalk, he took my limp palm as if we were shaking hands: "I'll make y'a deal, sonny. I'll make 'em eighteen inches!"

At my bar mitzvah a month later, I looked like I had gone up to our stifling attic and put on one of my father's old suits—big padded shoulders, oversized pants up to my chest, and enormous cuffs that fell like living room drapes around my shiny black shoes. All day I felt like a boy in a man's clothes, not a vision of coolness like Philip Gaynor. And that night I hung the suit in my closet and never again took it off the hanger.

For more than thirty years after that defining day, I occasionally tried to go out and buy another "good suit." To be a man. But each time I walked into a department store, I turned away when I saw the staid selection of dark suits on the rack. I simply did not feel old enough to fit comfortably into them. As a teacher, I got by with the usual tweedy-corduroy-patches-on-the-elbows look. As a writer I got by with considerably less. And in all that time—while high school, college, marriage, and the births of seven children whisked by like telephone poles from a speeding train—despite all the trappings of manhood, including my share of gray and missing hair, there were still moments when I felt exactly like the boy who stood on that riser, when anticipation could make me feel as if I was soaring through the air like Duke Snider climbing the wall at Ebbets Field; when my powerlessness would make me a shrinking observer of my own unfulfilled destiny. There still are those moments.

A few years ago, though, with a wedding to attend and a graduation speech to give, I could no longer avoid the inevitable. I plodded forlornly in and out of several men's departments in the local mall, burdened with the knowledge that nothing was ever going to feel right. At the last store, just as I picked another disappointing suit off the rack, I spied an older salesman in a gray suit approaching from behind the counter. The pants sloshed around his brown shoes.

"Try it on . . . just for size," he called out.

"It won't fit," I mumbled, slipping my hand into the silk inner sleeve. At the wedding, I felt like I was going to the prom. After the graduation speech, I ripped off the jacket as if it was made of mail and went to a party full of eighteen-year-olds. I am not a man like my father was a man.

Put me in front of a class, behind a rototiller, underneath a sleeping baby, on top of a leaking roof—and I feel like a man. Let me read you a poem, plunge your toilet, rock you to sleep, yell at you for being out past curfew, hold you close, be your lover. I have known enough of life and death, ecstasy and despair, the suffocating heat of love, the bone-knocking chill of loneliness, to know my solidly fragile place as a man in this world.

Put me in a suit, though, "Just for size," and I still shrink like all men do in freezing streams, a little boy out in the big cold world.

The X Chromosome
and *Being True to*
Your Real Self

> What is most beautiful in virile men is something
> feminine; what is most beautiful in feminine women
> is something masculine.
>
> —Susan Sontag,
> *Against Interpretation*

On the wall behind me is a framed poster made
by Louisa Melo for the 1994 New Paltz High
School girls' soccer team homecoming game. In
bold caps it reads, "LOOK OUT FOR CLOVER,
SHE'LL RUN YOU OVER." And in the center is a
most interesting variation on a satyr, an illustra-
tion of a bulldozer with the head of a girl in a
ponytail. That's Clover.

It's hard to believe, but our sweet, lovely, lithe
little daughter—a girl whose bedroom is cluttered
with hundreds of cuddly stuffed animals—would
knock you down and trample you with her cleats
if she wanted the ball—or whatever happens to
roll in front of her—badly enough at the moment.
But it is absolutely true.

I was thinking about that old poster because we just got back from trick-or-treating—an interesting turn of events, when the most powerless people in the community band together for one day to extort candy from their adult oppressors. Walking into the quiet house, I realized once again that nothing is ever quite as it seems. Bay, whose hands are already bigger than a bear's paws, and who is more patently macho than anyone in the family—fists high in the air as he does a victory lap after scoring a goal in soccer—dressed up as a prom queen for Halloween this year. (Actually, he was quite cute.) And perhaps even more remarkable than his brief dallying into the confusing world of the cross-dresser, Bay simply does not understand aggression. Unlike Sister Terminator, Clover, he never runs over anyone in soccer, basketball, baseball, or street hockey. In fact, he never hits anyone, not even when they've belted him first.

Which is more than I can say about Elizabeth, nine years old and all of forty-seven pounds, a little girl in flippy floppy pigtails who scoffs at the crudeness of boys of all ages and has never met a dress she didn't like. She belted Bay with an impressive roundhouse the other day when he had the gall to refuse to listen to her instructions about a game of Chinese Checkers. Elizabeth is so delicate and fine-boned that when I grasp her upper arm, I can easily touch the tip of my thumb to the end of my middle finger, yet she sent Mr. Macho reeling against the cinderblock wall in the basement. (Of course, he didn't hit her back.)

Patti and I have obviously confused our children somewhere along the way. I'm pretty sure they started out okay: our little guys have known how to go *vroom-vroom* with their Tonka trucks since they were old enough to sit up in their playpens— and throw the dolls we put in over the sides. And our little girls have known how to cuddle a doll baby or a stuffed alligator since they were old enough to understand that a Tonka truck could be rolled out of sight and out of mind with a gentle push.

But something must have gone wrong later on, when their hormones kicked in. Addie is, pound for pound, the strongest person in the family. The girl's biceps, which she sometimes refers to as "guns," are as hard as the thick steel cables on sus-pension bridges. Cael, who is as big as a bear and has no inter-est in aesthetics whatsoever, except as they rhyme with athletics, went out and bought a house—a nest!—years before he was even married. Nancy is the only person in the family who actually understands logarithms, despite the myth that higher mathematics is supposedly a male-only domain. And Danny, who sometimes smells like a bear and says things like "Chicks dig me," closes his door and writes the most tender and sensitive poetry in the house.

Woe is us. In a world where politicians and radio talk show hosts—who are increasingly the same person—tell us that gen-der confusion is going to be the ruination of this culture, we've allowed our children to be who they are, regardless of expecta-tions. Depending on whose political ox is being gored, which is perhaps an unwise but apt choice of metaphors, our kids are apparently going to hell in a pink handbasket dangled by whiny males in short shorts *or* they're on a death march from the Upper Peninsula of Michigan in front of goose-stepping chauvinists dragging their hog-tied—and high-heeled—women behind them.

As David Spade from *Saturday Night Live* used to say, "I don't think so."

All this talk of gender confusion is quite absurd, as Bay or Elizabeth can easily explain to you, especially when the real differences between the sexes is so self-evident. Think about it. (As my mother said to me forty-seven years ago when I asked in a three-year-old nap-induced stupor how people told the dif-ference between boy babies and girl babies, "Think about it.")

And if thinking about it is too taxing—and like me, you slept through Mr. Lineweaver's engaging tenth grade biology lec-ture on genes—here's the skinny direct from Webster's: "... *in most animals, including man* [sic], *all the eggs carry an X chromo-some and the spermatozoa either an X or Y chromosome, and an egg receiving an X chromosome at birth will develop into a female (XX) while one receiving a Y will develop into a male (XY)."*

Which seems unquestionably reasonable: men and women,

boys and girls, are fundamentally the same (the first X's) and fundamentally different (the second X or Y). No one has ever confused Nancy with Cael or Bay for Elizabeth. In fact, not a soul at the New Paltz Halloween parade down Main Street failed to recognize Bay underneath his wig and prom dress. (Maybe the lumbering flat-footed stride gave him away.)

There's a picture of Addie in one of the family albums that seems to sum it up for me: She's around three or four, wearing a smudged little smock dress and standing in the middle of the rural lane where we used to live. In one hand is a baseball glove, and dangling by the hair in the other hand is her favorite dolly.

That's the way it is, and so that's the way it's gotta be. And I like it just fine.

Xmas:
The Power of Faith

> People can't concentrate properly on blowing other / people to pieces properly if their minds are poisoned / by thoughts suitable to the twenty-fifth of De- / cember.
>
> —Ogden Nash,
> *Merry Christmas, Nearly Everybody!*

Back in what might pass as polyestered memories of the fifties on Long Island, it seemed to my outer child that all those wonderfully tacky Christmas decorations would suddenly appear each year as if by divine intervention at 12:01 A.M. on the Friday morning after another gluttonous Thanksgiving eve. And on Saturday morning we could pick up our glossy calendars from the neighborhood dry cleaners, listen to Perry Como's standard Yuletide favorites on the AM dial, begin the tantalizing daily shopping countdowns to Christmas, and watch the Amatos—the lone Catholic family in our suburban Jewish neighborhood—brighten up the entire development with their twinkling lights.

It was wonderful and magical, indeed a true spiritual experience for this non-Gentile. (And it was right on time.)

These days, however, with thick Christmas season catalogs arriving in bulk right after Labor Day, and big chain stores beginning their advertising and decorating campaigns for Christmas before we've washed the ghosts of Halloween off the windows, it seems that the season has lost some of its glow. Even more amazing to this wandering Jew, the multicultural landscape from Paramus, New Jersey, to Pasadena, California, is speckled red and green with Christmas shops open 365 days a year. And what about those twinkling little white lights? Once reserved exclusively for the Christmas season, they now make chichi restaurants and upscale shops glimmer all year round. (Just for the record, I don't want to leave out some of my neighbors in the Hudson Valley who never actually take their Christmas lights down from the year before; they just plug 'em in again sometime in November.)

At this point, I guess I'm supposed to bemoan the crass commercialism of contemporary society, the intrusion of the profane dollar into the sacred season of belief, the undoing of family values everywhere—and perhaps put in a good word for Hanukkah and Kwanzaa. But if you've read this far, you know that my sympathies don't often lie with the way things are supposed to go. I prefer to celebrate what is real, what actually touches our lives, what truly brings all of us together, what finally gives us faith in the redemptive nature of the universe.

And nothing quite brings my family together like the Christmas holidays. In the middle of the deep and dark woods at the base of the Shawangunk Mountains, the big house shimmers like a star from the glistening smiles and heightened pulses, as wanderers, every one of us, seek shelter and warmth under one big sloping snow-covered roof. This year Addie will travel in from New Orleans. Danny will soar in from Wisconsin. Nancy and Clover will drive up from Chapel Hill, North Carolina. Cael and Melissa will sleigh up from Durham.

Two Decembers ago on Christmas Eve, we all gathered behind the last of our "babies," Bay and Elizabeth, looking out at the starry sky where first Elizabeth, then Bay, actually spotted the sleigh—THE SLEIGH—whooshing across the heavens.

Elizabeth, at seven, was completely charmed, a smile of grace twinkling across that wonderful face. And Bay, who was ten and probably too old to really believe that Santa could possibly be sailing past the stars, pressed his stubby finger against the cold window and yelled, "I see 'im! I see 'im! I see 'im!" as if he really did.

Frankly I don't know whether Bay was just being kind to the little sister whom he both loves and loathes with all his big heart—or whether he thought he actually saw the sleigh. I don't care. Magic occurred in what we all shared standing there behind our two innocents. To his great credit, Danny kept his big-brotherly cynicism to himself. But Nancy, who was twenty-two at the time and just beginning to understand what is truly mystical, stepped up and said she saw it, too. Then Clover pouted that she must have missed it. And Addie asked what it looked like.

Which was when Elizabeth told us *exactly* what it looked like. And we all knew she had seen the sleigh whooshing across the starry sky as clearly as we saw joy in her glistening eyes.

Faith indeed comes in different forms—and each kind provides its own rather wonderful form of redemption, especially around Christmas, when practically everyone is a true believer. Which is the reason, despite the understandable wish of bumper stickers imploring all of us to keep the Christ in Christmas, my pulse races, my cheeks burn North Pole red, and my arms transform into wings when I see the utterly commercialized Xmas designation on billboards and mall signs up and down Route 9.

I have come to hope with every ounce of goodwill alive in my soul that everybody in the universe spends all their real—and funny—money on gaudily wrapped presents for the innocent and faithful who live among us. For if we spend every last red cent, there will be no cash left to buy another gun or tank or bomb to shoot down the faithful countenance of children, their noses pressed to the window glass.

While some profoundly misguided parents around this dizzying globe actually disown their children over profoundly fallible notions of faith and trust, and others in the universal family massacre each other daily over absurd distinctions between one vision of God and another, I'd rather take the generic X path and light the bright lights, sing the beautiful songs, eat the cookies, drink the nog, and celebrate the birth of babies into the family of human beings made in the image of their gods.

We're mongrels, we Lewi. A scroungy band of Christians, Jews, Agnostics, Atheists, True Believers, and Pagan Idol Worshippers, we travel once a year—for a whole year—like unarmed Bedouins across the mountains and rivers, swamps and deserts, of this land, following the stars to give homage to the miracle of infancy everywhere in the universe. We put the X in Christmas wherever we go. It is the signature of the uninformed, the unenlightened, the innocent. The ones who know that there is always a sleigh drifting across the sky all year long for those who allow children to show them the way home.

Y

Youthfulness:
Forgiveness for the Passage of Time

> The passing moment is all we can be sure of; it is only common sense to extract its utmost value from it; the future will one day be the present and will seem as unimportant as the present now does.
> —W. Somerset Maugham,
> *The Summing Up*

Last winter, snow burying the flowerpots on the back deck, I was flipping through old summer photographs and wistfully recalling the breezy untouched paradise that Hatteras Island, North Carolina, used to be. Then I turned to last year's glossy Kodaks and lamented that everything was changing. Too many people. Too many cars. Too many cottages behind the dunes. Jet Skis on the Sound. Go-cart tracks. Surfers.

Unfortunately, I was babbling out loud, and eight-year-old Elizabeth was leaning over my hunched shoulders looking at the pictures with me. I craned my neck around to see her sweet face, but rather than nodding in agreement, I saw behind her pressed lips a mirror of the same confusion and anger I once knew more than forty years ago while enduring uncles' droning accounts of the glorious twenties and thirties. In that instant I recalled vividly how the old men's chins receded into their jowls as they threw accusations like gauntlets at my feet. How they muttered on about how jaded and immoral my cherished world had become. And I tasted that old shame again; felt my eyes fixed on the floor, just like Elizabeth was doing right then.

Not knowing where to go with my unhappiness, I fixed my eyes on the snapshots of our first year on the Outer Banks, ten years before Elizabeth was born. In 1978, Hatteras was little more than a narrow and raw barrier island situated stubbornly between the rough Atlantic and the Great Dismal Swamp: vast empty beaches, shifting sands, sea oats, and a few scrub pines from ocean to Pamlico Sound. It lacked all the electricity of the Jersey Shore; it had none of the pretentious charm of Martha's Vineyard or Amagansett. Our weathered boxy cottage on salt-treated pilings offered little more than protection from the wind and mosquitoes, an unobscured access to the beach, and no phone and no TV. The closest grocery store with fresh vegetables was forty-five minutes away in Kill Devil Hills; the closest hospital, a speeding hour and a half to Elizabeth City. In fact, the way of life back then could be summed up by the slogan on the Jobob's Trading Post T-shirt:

IF IT'S WORTH BUYING, WE MIGHT HAVE IT

By 1988, though—the year of Elizabeth's birth—things started to change on an island that once seemed resiliently unchangeable. Rolling into Rodanthe at dusk in the Lewis VW Clownmobile, we were stunned to see street signs with typical beachy names stuck in the deep sand along Route 12. Despite the fact that they were promptly blown down by the ever-bellowing wind—or shot off by the ever-bellowing locals—progress was indeed at hand. And soon enough, a condo and a time-share broke ground in Waves; and thereafter a charming shopping plaza named Rodanthe Station was erected downwind from the pier. The owners of the local rickety waterslide added a new "Can-Am" go-cart track. Expensive multileveled beach homes began to dot the area behind the dunes. Two more summers passed, and New York plates became frequent enough that we no longer honked or waved when we passed. A big modern Food Lion opened just eighteen miles down the road in Avon. Emily's, previously an all-you-can-eat fried everything restaurant in Waves, was renovated: shiny brass, raw oysters, fresh tuna and wahoo, service by "waitpersons," and a list of 120 domestic and imported beers. The Hatteras Marina down at the end of the island introduced sushi right alongside the bologna and beef jerkies.

The drive off the island last August was congested, nearly as frustrating as it used to be leaving Cape Cod on Sunday afternoons in the early seventies. We returned to the horrendous traffic on Main Street in New Paltz, the crowded classrooms at the local elementary schools, the subdivisions built atop former orchards and hayfields. We returned to rising taxes, volatile anger at town meetings, dairy farms closing all over the region, suits by environmentalists, the entrepreneurial excitement of developers and weekenders closing in on our way of life. We returned to the traditional American stubbornness in the faces of my neighbors, who will not be told what they can or can't do with their land. Just like Hatteras.

So when Elizabeth turned and walked away in silence following her old man's harangue, I also felt the loneliness that my uncles must have known in their overwhelming disappointment with modern life in the fifties. And I returned alone to the packet of photos from last summer. I peered deeply into those gorgeous tanned faces on the beach, picture after picture, searching for some evidence that I was right. That, indeed, my uncles were right. That everything was changing for the worse.

But I would have had to have been blind not to see the utter joy in my little girl's eyes in one bright moment as she glanced back from the immutable blue-green ocean and laughed out loud into the time-stopping lens. How could I not see the divine serenity in the picture of Clover floating out beyond the breakers? the eternal silliness of Addie squealing as she held a jellyfish at arm's length? the infinite lure of love in Nancy and Michael holding each other close on an empty beach? the suddenly very married-looking Cael and Melissa?

Flipping through the rest of those glossy memories, the glory of an ordinary family vacation spread out like big blankets across the vast dunes, it seemed as if the kids had again had the summer of their lives. I nodded. So had I.

So when I turned to yet another album from another lost year, I was not surprised that the children there showed me—page after page after glorious page of the same beach, the same waving sea oats, the same arc of sky and water in the distance—that our lives change all the time, regardless of what we desire. Nothing stays the same.

In living truth, the past is too often a fiction, a caricature of memory with which an older generation, unhappy with the ordinary imperfect present, recalls halcyon days when everything was pure and right. Just as my uncles did to me. Just as I did to Elizabeth. As much as we might wish for a purity that never existed in our cherished pasts, the problems of living well in the inescapable present continue to propel us into the future.

It is obvious to me that as caretakers of our children and the earth that they inherit, we must act vigilantly to counter the thoughtless devastation of our natural resources by those who are too greedy or evil to see beyond their own empty existences. But to lament that life in the beautiful Shawangunk Mountains or Hatteras Island or New York City in the late 1990s no longer looks or feels like it once did in a vaguely remembered past is, in itself, another kind of greed. It is a form of evil that dooms each generation to the plague of discontent.

With the next century a few rolls of film away, I'm certain that the worst legacy we could leave Elizabeth and her friends is not the intrepid advances of a society that grows and changes in spite of itself, but to keep telling them—as we were told—that change is bad, that the past was better, "how good it used to be." Soon enough they'll come to believe it.

If our children are to save the earth—and I believe they are—they must cherish it first.

You Scratch My Back, I'll Scratch Yours:
Paying Your Own Way

> *Compromise*, n. Such an adjustment of conflicting interests as gives each adversary the satisfaction of thinking he has got what he ought not to have, and is deprived of nothing except what was justly his due.
> —Ambrose Bierce,
> *The Devil's Dictionary*

I may be carbon dating myself, but I do remember a lost golden era when a good old-fashioned twenty-minute back rub would cost me a quarter—or, if the masseur or masseuse was older and thus more accomplished and savvy, the price would rise to the exorbitant rate of fifty cents.

Of course, my personal trainers in those long-gone days were between the ages of six and nine, and twenty minutes of each one's hand strength, knowledge of human physiology, and concentration quotient produced at full capacity what might be the equivalent of a seven-second Swedish massage. Yet, even at the highly inflationary rate of fifty cents, twenty minutes of a moderately unsatisfactory back rub was still a good deal, if only because of the weight on the small of my aching back. And sometimes I could trick them into sitting there for an additional ten minutes by having them make stubby fingertip "drawings." (I would then try in vain to guess what was drawn, and then the unwitting illustrator would have to redo his or her body artwork.)

Anyway, I was always pleased. And what's more, the proprietors of the mobile back rub clinic were invariably pleased with their earnings. First Cael, then Nancy, and then Addie stumbled along to micromanage the professional corporation of domestic kneaders for a price, pocketing the proceeds in their jeans (and generally losing them to the couch mouth before the night was through). In addition, on family holidays, when my own children were on vacation from Dad's aching back, my nieces Anne and Isabel were eager entrepreneurs of the art.

However, since the day that Addie realized—somewhere around age nine—that she could make more money in less time mowing lawns and breaking rocks, my days of employing child labor were suddenly over. Clover has never aspired to the capitalist notion of work for hire, and Danny, who learned passive aggression early and well, priced himself right out of the market before he was certified to work on the old man's back. And more recently, Bay and Elizabeth became the first Americans to take Nancy Reagan's advice seriously. They "just say no" and turn back to the television. In fact, they often have the unmitigated gall to ask me to massage their backs. And so does Clover. And, of course, they want me to do it for free.

Which brings me to the heart of the matter of family values: everything comes with a price. "You scratch my back and I'll scratch yours" is not an empty phrase. In real family life, there is no free ride. You want something, then you have to give something in return. There are absolutely no entitlements except eternal love, a quality that can't be bought, sold, bartered, optioned, or auctioned, regardless of your desire to amend, enlarge, quantify, or even sever it. As such, eternal love is the only commodity that's worthless when you really want something from someone in your family.

Everything else is game. Whether it's a meal that is paid for by a simple expression of thanks or your turn to clear the table or wash the dishes—or it's a ride from a brother to town or a secret that must be guarded—there is always an ounce or a pound of spirit to be forked over. The most destructive element in any family of any size or constitution is what the late psychoanalyst Karen Horney called "claims." Claims are akin to staking out emotional or material territory on the basis of nothing more than who you are. For example, you may think that because you are pretty or smart or lost a game or have been sick or did something nice for someone in 1988, you *deserve* to have your back scratched without the obligation of scratching someone else's back. You think it's your due. It's not.

In a perfect world—which would certainly be the most imperfect solution to the world's problems—family members would happily give freely of their time and energy to each other, smiles on their bright faces, fully content in the knowledge that it is better to give than to receive. And, of course, receive they would, because everybody would be so busy giving. In a perfect world, you would never have to say please. Or pretty please. Or be so crass as to have to fork over some hard-earned coins for your pleasure.

These days, with not a soul around willing to scratch my back—even if I scratch theirs—I have learned another lesson about family values (gleaned from Mick Jagger and his ancient Stones): You can't always get what you want . . . but you get what you need. In lieu of massaging my back, Patti got me a membership to the local health club, where I am supposed to stretch and strengthen these aching muscles, not knead them.

At the health club, where we pay fifty dollars a month so that I can pour every ounce of energy and sweat into going absolutely nowhere on an uncompromisingly stationary Stairmaster, I have come to appreciate more fully what a good deal I had back in the good old days: a perfect deal, according to Bierce. Completely bereft of small, dirty, greedy hands to knead me into someone as happy as Pillsbury Doughboy, I climb to the top of Mount Zero as penance for being such a cheapskate back when the going was so good.

Z

Zero Tolerance:
Trite but True Prescriptive Priorities

> Think of me as I am, nothing extenuate . . . then you must think of one that loved not wisely but too well.
>
> —William Shakespeare,
> *Othello*

Clover called home recently to tell us about her participation in the "Take Back the Night" march at the University of North Carolina. She was invigorated, resolute, justly proud of her participation in the angry demonstration protesting male violence against women.

I felt like I'd eaten something rotten. I listened to her impassioned voice, wondering how we have come to the point in this country where our daughters must be afraid of walking the streets at night in college towns like idyllic Chapel Hill. On what feverish day did we accept the infectious notion that independent young women need bodyguards to go from the dorm to the library? My throat grew parched and raw. I wanted to cry out, but was struck silent with a form of laryngitis of the soul.

Behind my tongue is a crowded apothecary of parental clichés swallowed over the past half-century; old saws like "Boys will be boys" and "Spare the rod and spoil the child." As a writer and teacher, I try to keep those worn bromides hidden in the damp uvular darkness, but as a father of seven children who daily finds himself at a loss for words in the incomprehensively perilous world of the nineties, it is often one of those trite sayings that saves me from the despairing silence.

After hanging up the phone, I wandered through the darkened house, peering into the empty bedrooms of two other daughters who are also at college, one whose resilient core was splintered several years ago by the threat of a boy's violence, another whose friend's jaw was shattered by a young man who supposedly loved her. I thought about two of my adult students at Empire State College whose ex-husbands battered them for years. And when my throat grew so tight I couldn't breathe, the only thing I managed to cough up was the hackneyed "Boys should never hit girls."

It doesn't get said much anymore, no doubt because of its simplistic chauvinism that some might say insults both males and females. But I heard that phrase often while growing up in the suburban fifties. There was nothing relative about it, nothing situational, nothing ambiguous. Nothing cute. Nothing that would inspire politically correct apologies. Simply, there was nothing more despicable than a boy who would hit a girl.

Of course, it is naive to think that because forty years ago we were told not to hit girls, boys did not grow into men who battered women. Yet it does seem that violence against females has become endemic in this country since my childhood. Every day I turn away from the nauseatingly entertaining evening news—another day, another woman assaulted—knowing that each of my seven children is a potential victim of this horrid disease as it metastasizes its way across the country. And the prognosis is often fatal: women die and men who batter females rarely get well.

So I went downstairs with my finger pointed like a hypodermic needle at eleven-year-old Bay and eight-year-old Elizabeth. "Boys should never hit girls!" I barked.

Elizabeth, who already knows what it's like to be smaller and not as strong as the boys in her second grade class, looked at me like I'd finally woken up. And Bay, who is a sweet boy, merely shrugged and nodded in agreement, and then turned back to his computer game. He hadn't hit anyone, boy or girl, and as such it didn't mean much to him. But it cleared my throat and my head, and I do know that he heard me.

After nearly three decades of parenting, I know I'm supposed to put expectations in context, to make moral and ethical pronouncements relevant to the child's immediate experiences. But in a world that is as profoundly ill as ours, I think we're now beyond that kind of polite family psychology.

From this night forward, my children, young and old, will hear that phrase often. It will acquire the same metrical memory as *an apple a day* . . . or *a stitch in time*. . . . It will sit like a time-released aspirin dissolving on the tips of their tongues, poised to combat whatever fever comes their way. It will linger in the damp uvular darkness of their own imperfect adulthoods as a vaccine so that they might bark out the same tried-and-true home remedy to my unborn grandchildren: *Boys should never hit girls.*

Failing to speak such a simple, timeworn truth *every day in every way*, we might as well lock the doors and go to bed. And Clover and her brave friends will never take back the night.

Zeal:
The Final Word

> Let a man in a garret but burn with enough intensity and he will set fire to the world.
> —Antoine de Saint-Exupéry,
> *Wind, Sand, and Stars*

Cael was simply dumbfounded that his father was acting like an irresponsible teenager—although he was not necessarily surprised. After nearly twenty-seven years of a neoclassic case of Wordsworth's *The child is father of the man*, nothing comes as much of a shock to either of us.

In my defense, however, emotions were intense, zealous, contagious, buzzing with the electrical currents of the heavens in those daylight hours before my oldest son's wedding to the fair Melissa in St. Petersburg, Florida. In fact, I was so wired up all morning that I couldn't bear to hang around the hotel and all the relatives for a minute longer, so I took a motley crew of pasty-faced, library-legged young and old Yankees in last summer's shorts across the street to a spring training game at Al Lang Field—the Cards versus the A's.

Cael, it turns out, in the midst of the ionized anticipation of the rest of his life, apparently went from calmly disbelieving to cloudy and annoyed to thunderous rage to lightning snapping limbs and trees bending in hurricane-force gales as the minutes approached for all of us to leave for the chapel. According to Patti he was pacing back and forth in the hotel room, spitting into the generational wind and cursing the fates for having been born to a father whose raft never quite made it to the main stream. As he stood there, hands raised to the heavens, he was no doubt wondering if it was even remotely possible—or probable—that I was going to strand him there on third base.

I didn't. Of course not. I'm not quite as adrift as some of my children fear, although I did have to race ahead of the motley crew back to the hotel after a called strike three to end the seventh inning, bursting through the door with just enough time to slide into the tux and sprint down the line to the wedding.

To move the combined baseball-weather metaphor along, Patti had on her game face, intense and focused on the job at hand, despite the stormy conditions along the entire Gulf Coast. Elizabeth was as silly as a waterspout and flushed with anticipation of "stealing the show" (as she so unaffectedly sputtered the day she got her flower girl dress), jabbering nonsensically and nonstop like a third base coach until the wedding ceremony itself, when she nearly lost her voice.

As did her big brother Cael, though not his nerve, his raspy "I do" barely audible in the emotion-filled sanctuary. They were perhaps the most courageous two words I've ever heard in my life. Never mind what our leaders, social scientists, and lexicographers say about bravery; for an ordinary person—and we are all at heart profoundly ordinary people—marriage may be the most daring and bold act that woman or man can hope to perform. Simply put, there is no other time in our lives when we so completely—so thoughtfully—so passionately—so purposefully—and so fearfully devote our lives to something larger than ourselves.

It is a brazen affirmation of life, in many ways far more audacious than committing oneself to work, which is almost always a devil's deal. More audacious than going to war, which holds the lure of martyrdom. More audacious than conception, which we are, often in spite of ourselves, driven by nature to accomplish. Even those of us who give ourselves wholly over to God are not taking such an audacious leap; to give up the world for eternal peace and salvation may be right, but is not necessarily as daring as binding yourself to another's existence "for better or worse, in sickness and in health, 'til death do you part." I get the shivers just typing those words.

Yes, some people perform great heroic feats in their lives, like running into burning houses to save children or diving on top of live grenades to save their compatriots. But there are no medals for a good marriage, no sainthood bestowed upon its members, no annual stipend, just the promise of a common journey away from the "What if's" of childhood, full of hope and despair, love and loneliness, aching and aging.

Wow.

Which is why I'm sure people cry at weddings. We may love the romance, but we recognize the bravery. So I wept heartily at Cael and Melissa's wedding, although blubbered might be a more accurate adjective. Seeing our firstborn up at the altar with his serenely beautiful partner through life, Melissa, all I kept remembering was the weight of him in my arms as I rocked him to sleep twenty-six years before; the look and feel of my toddler in his OshKosh overalls, those stubby little Keds running along the sidewalk in Milwaukee. And now that soft and unbelievably sweet little boy was over six feet and about to turn the corner, never to be seen in the same light again.

Of course Patti misted up, but she has more self-control than I do. And I saw Clover get a little squishy, and a few of the bridesmaids with eyes pooling; grandparents with handkerchiefs out and wet; sniffles all around the white sanctuary. The usual. However, Elizabeth cried and couldn't stop; not because she was unhappy, but because of all the dreams of a little girl's days and nights that went into her long, glorious, flowered walk down the aisle, which ended so precipitously at the altar.

Patti's sister Leigh also could not stop crying; and not because she was unhappy, not because of unspoken regrets or broken promises. But because the zealous fire of her nephew's bravery, the first of the cousins to make the leap into the darkness, would undoubtedly light the way for the rest to follow. And they would all eventually move along—celebrating the starting all over again—leaving us behind as is good and right.

That's why people cry at weddings. That's why people get drunk. That's why people cry and dance and get drunk and say things that they'd never say at any other time in their lives: the simple vision of two people standing at the gates of marriage is stunning. It demands powerful feelings. Zeal. Champagne. Contagion. Brush fires here; brush fires there.

A spark ignited the heart of Cael's lifelong friend Scott Sherman, who was so fired up by the ceremony that he decided then and there that he had to marry as well. And not only that, it had to be a Lewis girl. So he got down on one knee and proposed to Nancy, who clung tight to her boyfriend Mike's arm. Then he asked Addie, who told her boyfriend Nate to save her honor. Then Clover, who smiled and said, "Ask my mom." Which he did, and she fortunately turned him down, choosing the old immature model over the new immature inebriated one.

As Elizabeth was already asleep up in the hotel room, the intrepid knight errant moved up a generation and asked my eighty-four-year-old mother for her hand. "I just want a Lewis girl," he moaned. She asked him what for. That was too deep a question, so he turned to the next closest thing, a Lewis cousin, Isabel, who was at the wedding with her longtime friend Lyle. Undaunted, our Don Quixote de la Manhattan staggered ahead and pledged his undying love to the fair Dulcinea del Burton, promising in the last few moments of stuporous clarity that he'd duel Lyle for the honor of her hand.

That night Patti and I held onto each other for dear life. We held each other to honor ourselves and our little boy, and our new daughter. We held each other, the breathing of babies in the background, to reaffirm our vows, to start again at the beginning, to be picked up by the riffling winds, to soar beyond the furthest edge where anyone can go alone.

And ten months later, when Cael called to say that Melissa was pregnant, we knew we were where we had to be.

Be zealous.